Nicky Hooks and Sharon Burnett (who although not quite a gestalt entity are in fact joined at the hip) met in 1983 when Sharon moved from Dagenham to Braintree in Essex and started work at the same branch of a certain supermarket. In 1991 Nicky finally succumbed to Sharon's constant nagging and thinking, 'Anything for a quiet life,' decided to watch Series IV of *Red Dwarf*. Needless to say, she soon became hooked. After watching two episodes of Series VI being recorded, Nicky decided the time had come to quiz Sharon on her extensive knowledge of Rimmer, Lister and co., and so the first hundred questions were born. Several rounds later they realized how much they had enjoyed being tested and thought that other 'Smeggies' would find a quiz book devoted to *Red Dwarf* just as entertaining as they had. They then approached the programme's creators, Rob Grant and Doug Naylor, and the rest, as they say, is history.

THE RED DWARF
QUIZ BOOK

NICKY HOOKS AND SHARON BURNETT

PENGUIN BOOKS

PENGUIN BOOKS

Published by the Penguin Group
Penguin Books Ltd, 27 Wrights Lane, London W8 5TZ, England
Penguin Books USA Inc., 375 Hudson Street, New York, New York 10014, USA
Penguin Books Australia Ltd, Ringwood, Victoria, Australia
Penguin Books Canada Ltd, 10 Alcorn Avenue, Toronto, Ontario, Canada M4V 3B2
Penguin Books (NZ) Ltd, 182–190 Wairau Road, Auckland 10, New Zealand

Penguin Books Ltd, Registered Offices: Harmondsworth, Middlesex, England

First published 1994
1 3 5 7 9 10 8 6 4 2

For the photographs on the questionnaires, the authors and publisher
gratefully acknowledge Michael Brooks (p. 71), Nobby Clark
(pp. 129 and 130) and Mike Vaughan (pp. 9, 29, 75, 85 and 109)

Filmset by Datix International Limited, Bungay, Suffolk
Printed in England by Clays Ltd, St Ives plc
Set in 11/14 pt Monophoto Bembo

To Mark and Andy

INVENTORY

Inventory

Inventory

ACKNOWLEDGEMENTS

Our many thanks to Rob Grant, Doug Naylor, Charles Armitage, Kate Williams, Helen Norman and Kate Cotton. Also to Chris Barrie, Craig Charles, Danny John-Jules, Robert Llewellyn, Hattie Hayridge and Norman Lovett. Special thanks to Vanessa Bays for her much valued contribution and to Patricia Ratnage for putting up with us both for the past millennium, and for having complete faith in us from the very beginning.

With fond memories of the memory of Joanne Locke.

N. H. and S. B.

Are you good enough to enter
Space Corps Academy, or are you
an inch below regulation height?

or

THE QUESTIONS

SMEG!

Even 'Thicky' Holden should be able to answer this lot!

1 Name Rimmer's brothers.
2 Who collects singing potatoes?
3 Who has a bum like 'two badly parked Volkswagens'?
4 Who was Kryten's replacement?
5 Who removed Lister's second appendix?
6 Name Lister's goldfish.
7 How many hours WOO did Rimmer inflict on the rest of the crew?
8 Which floor was the stasis leak on?
9 What affliction did Kryten's spare head suffer from?
10 What did Rimmer suggest 'jigsaw' might mean?
11 Who did Juanita Chicata have an affair with?
12 Who was the sexiest computer sprite?
13 How much did Talkie Toaster cost?
14 Where did Lister want to buy a farm?
15 What was the 'Quagaar' capsule really?
16 What were Rimmer and Kryten known as on the Backwards Planet?
17 Who did Rimmer's beehive make him look like?
18 What is Lister's favourite music?
19 Why did Rimmer say he couldn't wear the escort boots?
20 How many Apocalypse Boys are there?

21 What was Lister's address in Better Than Life?

22 Whose breast did Rimmer 'acquire'?

23 Who was Captain Paxo?

24 When is Gazpacho Soup Day?

25 What did Lister used to go 'scrumping' for?

26 Who watches *Die Screaming with Sharp Things in Your Head*?

27 What sound does a cat make when he traps his sexual organs in something?

28 In which locker did Lister live on Mimas Central Shuttle Station?

29 What did the Gelfs want in exchange for the O/G Unit?

30 Who can open beer bottles with his overbite?

31 How many press-ups did Gandhi have to do?

32 Who is *Red Dwarf: Infinity Welcomes Careful Drivers* dedicated to?

33 Which channel has a hologram reading the news?

34 How long did Rimmer spend on Rimmerworld?

35 Which exam did Lister take in order to outrank Rimmer?

36 How many years into the future are the crew's future selves?

37 Where did Kochanski work?

38 What did Lister catch in the canal?

39 Who were the Cat's parents?

40 Who murdered Paranoia?

41 What did Lister spray under his arms by mistake instead of deodorant?

42 Who looked 'so geeky that he couldn't even get into a science fiction convention'?

43 What happens when the Cat gets excited?
44 Who is as 'dead as a can of Spam'?
45 Who was the first woman on the moon?
46 What did the black holes turn out to be?
47 Where was Rimmer born?
48 Name the Apocalypse Boys.
49 What did the Cat do with Lister's mind tape?
50 What was Rimmer's Space Mistress called?
51 What did the Psirens' victim use as a full stop?
52 What was referred to as a 'small off-duty Czechoslovakian traffic warden'?
53 Who stitched name tags on his ship's issue condoms?
54 What do 'BSC' and 'SSC' stand for?
55 Why did Bongo have a feeling that Ace had returned?
56 According to Rimmer's mother, what will Satan be going to work on when Rimmer becomes an officer?
57 Where did Kryten and Rimmer materialize on Wax World?
58 Who sings the *Red Dwarf* theme tune?
59 Who was the Cats' god?
60 What was the smallest grave on Rimmer's Psi-moon?
61 Who was William Doyle?
62 Which planet is Io a moon of?
63 Who would you fly to see on a magic carpet?
64 Which fragrance did Camille use?
65 Who was Queeg really?
66 What does Rimmer claim his middle name is?
67 Who played the part of Blaize Falconburger?
68 When encountering the Curry Monster, what did Rimmer suggest the crew make a surrender flag out of?

69 Which officer of the *Enlightenment* came aboard *Starbug*?
70 Who was a 'bitch queen from hell'?
71 What was Rimmer's one morning in the Samaritans known as?
72 What does Lister sweat?
73 How many years into deep space is *Red Dwarf* (approximately)?
74 What were engraved on Kryten's shooting irons?
75 What was referred to as a 'red-and-blue-striped golfing umbrella'?
76 When Lister woke up on Mimas, whose work permit did he say he had?
77 What did the Inquisitor think was the only purpose of existence?
78 What did the Quagaar warrior look like?
79 What did the Cat give Kryten as a present?
80 What is the only thing that can kill a vindaloo?
81 What is Grant Naylor's favourite colour?
82 In which situation would you perform a 'Half-Rimmer'?
83 Who was the 'rodent equivalent of Marlon Brando'?
84 Who plays Kochanski?
85 At what time did Kryten meet Camille at Parrot's?
86 Who was Captain Chloroform?
87 Name the ship's captain.
88 Why couldn't Kryten wear the Inquisitor's gauntlet?
89 What was the relationship between Sebastian and Billy Doyle?
90 What did Duane Dibbley's checklist comprise?
91 How long did Lister spend at art college?
92 How many days are there in a Mimian week?

93 What was Sheriff Kryten's mule called?

94 Who was the drummer with Smeg and the Heads?

95 How many days did Lister, the Cat and Kryten have to spend in quarantine?

96 Who would lose a 'battle of wits with a stuffed iguana'?

97 Where had Lister originally woken up on Mimas?

98 What was Lister's name when he was with Loretta?

99 According to the Cat, what would his middle name be if he had one?

100 Why did Holly choose to bring Rimmer back as a hologram?

101 What rank is Rimmer?

102 How long did it take Lister to make the foot of the Marilyn Monroe droid?

103 How do you get out of an Artificial Reality game?

104 What does 'GELF' stand for?

105 By how many inches did Lister's space mumps go down overnight?

106 If John, Frank and Howard were the Three Musketeers, who was Rimmer?

107 Which school did Rimmer go to?

108 What was Lister's job at Sainsbury's Megamarket?

109 According to Holly, what's a poor IQ for a glass of water?

110 What did Rimmer think Legion's light switch was?

111 What was the Cat's 'shiny thing'?

112 What is the Cat's third favourite activity?

113 How long had it been since Legion had had any visitors?

114 Who played Adolf Hitler in 'Timeslides'?

115 What can Hudzen do with his willy?

116 What did the crew need from the Gelfs?
117 How many times did Rimmer write 'I am a fish'?
118 Where did the 'Classic Wines' come from?
119 Who were the 'smart party'?

QUESTIONNAIRE

1) Full name. CHRISTOPHER JONATHAN BARRIE

2) Vital statistics. I'VE ONLY EVER MEASURED THE MIDDLE ONE AND THAT IS ANYTHING BETWEEN 32"-35" DEPENDING ON

3) Height. 5'11" HOW MUCH BEER I'VE HAD

4) Colour of eyes. HAZEL

5) Date of birth. 28/3/60

6) Place of birth. HANOVER, W. GERMANY

7) First job. LAWN MOWER OPERATOR, WYCOMBE DISTRICT COUNCIL, (SUMMER JOB '75)

8) First public appearance. FORGET WHERE, BUT I PLAYED A ROBIN IN A SCHOOL NATIVITY PLAY AGED ABOUT 5

9) First big break. JASPER CARROTT ELECTION SPECIAL '83

10) Ambition. TO KEEP WORKING

11) Hobbies. CLASSIC CARS ETC

12) If you could play any part, which part would you choose?
THE TITLE ROLE IN THAT FAMOUS MOVIE 'THE ADVENTURES OF THE MAN WHO LIES ON A BEACH IN THE SEYCHELLES & DOES BUGGER ALL BUT EAT, DRINK + SHAG.'

13) Favourite food/ drink. ANYTHING IN MODERATION, IT MIGHT BE A CLICHE BUT OYSTERS + CHAMPERS GOES DOWN WELL AS DOES A PINT OF BITTER + A DROP OF GOOD MALT WHISKEY

14) Favourite episode of Red Dwarf. MAROONED (SERIES 3) - GREAT YARN! DIMENSION JUMP (SERIES 4) (MOST ENJOYABLE TO DO)

15) Least favourite episode of Red Dwarf. BACKWARDS SEEMED FUN AT THE TIME, BUT LOOKING BACK AT IT, IT LOOKS A BIT TOO SILLY. IN DEMONS + ANGELS, MY COSTUME WAS BLOODY UNCOMFORTABLE

16) Favourite T.V. programme(s). VARIES RECENTLY, ONE FOOT IN THE GRAVE, LESS RECENTLY FAWLTY TOWERS, DAVID SUCHET'S 'POIROT' IS ENJOYABLE — ALL OF THESE, HOWEVER, PALE INTO INSIGNIFICANCE COMPARED TO NEWSROOM SOUTH EAST!

17) Favourite book. THE COMPLETE WORKS OF W. SHAKESPEARE MUST BE UP THERE, BUT WOULD THEY BE AS USEFUL AS THE AA CAR CARE HANDBOOK?

18) Favourite film. DIFFICULT TO SAY - BOND MOVIES + THE RAIDERS SERIES ARE FUN, DUEL (ANOTHER SPIELBERG) IS BRILLIANT, SOME LIKE IT HOT - CLASSIC BUT HOW CAN YOU LEAVE OUT CHITTY CHITTY BANG BANG?

19) Person you most admire, past or present. ONE OF THEM HAS TO BE GARY GLITTER (ANYONE WHO CAN GET AWAY WITH A RUG LIKE THAT FOR SO LONG MUST BE ADMIRABLE)

20) Inside leg measurement!!! 31" · ISH?

CROSSWORD 1
Rimmer

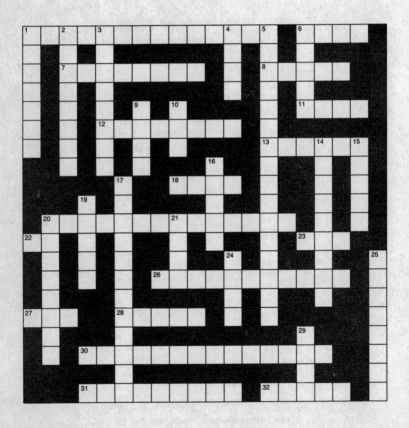

The Questions

Across

1 Rimmer is particularly interested in the twentieth-century variety of these (9,5)
6 Rimmer thinks he's one of these, five hundred times (4)
7 and 8 Rimmer's hologramatic lover (8,5)
11 Rimmer was given his first 'French' one of these by his Uncle Frank (4)
12 Rimmer's radio call sign (4,4)
13 The nickname of the inventor of the Tension Sheet (6)
18 You'll need this after eating some of Rimmer's dumplings! (4)
20 and 26 One of Rimmer's imaginary 'honours' (6,8,11)
22 Where Rimmer was born (2)
23 What a guy! (3)
26 See 20 across
27 A symptom of the holo-virus (3)
28 Rimmer's favourite musical instrument (5)
30 Rimmer's one and only sexual conquest (6,8)
31 Rimmer's been learning this for eight years (9)
32 Rimmer's middle name (5)

Down

1 Rimmer visited this city after eating freaky fungus (7)
2 The carrier of the holo-virus (8)
3 Rimmer's exclamation after having sex (8)
4 A 'short-term hormonal distraction' (4)
5 Rimmer's rank (6,10)
6 One of Rimmer's brothers (5)

 9 . . . .-virus (4)
10 The name of Rimmer's air hostess (3)
14 Rimmer's training officer (9)
15 The surname of the woman in Rimmer's imagined
    affair (5)
16 Rimmer has great difficulty with these (5)
17 25 November marks this day (8,4)
19 The surname of Sebastian and Billy (5)
20 Rimmer's nickname at school (8)
21 Dry white . . . . and Perrier (4)
24 Rimmer keeps a campaign book for this game (4)
25 What Rimmer is now that he is dead (8)
29 Rimmer's similarity to a can of Spam (4)

STAIRCASE 1

When the words listed below are placed horizontally and in the correct order within the grid, they will spell out diagonally (in the boxes marked in bold) another word from *Red Dwarf*.

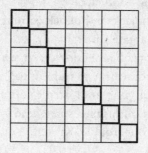

CAMILLE
CAPTAIN
GILBERT
HAMMOND
PARROTS
ROEBUCK
SILICON

WHO SAID THIS, AND WHERE?
Byte 1

State the characters in *Red Dwarf* who said the following, and in which episodes.

1 'It's my duty as a complete and utter bastard.'
2 'We'd better pray to God this works.'
3 'Smeg off, dog-food face.'
4 'I think I feel a Jackson Pollock coming on.'
5 'I look like Captain Emerald.'
6 'What's your problem – do you have a major luncheon appointment to rush off to?'
7 'You're a total smeg head, aren't you, Rimmer?'
8 'Well, get out of this one, smeg head.'
9 'You know your trouble, Kryten? You're a git.'
10 'Goodbyeee!'
11 'They only have to force me into platform shoes and flared trousers and I'll sing like Tweetie Pie.'
12 'All in all, today's been a bit of a bummer.'
13 'I stopped for quite a while, but I'm back on them now.'
14 'How do you turn this thing off, then?'
15 'Dream on, metal trash.'
16 'With respect, sir, you've got your head up your big fat arse.'
17 'All right, dudes, what's going down in Groove Town, then?'

18 'Souper.'

19 'Hi, honey; I'm home.'

20 'Swivel on it, punk.'

21 'This sounds like a twelve-change-of-underwear trip.'

22 'Why do I always have to be the strong one?'

23 'It's sort of like not as bad as a red alert, but a bit
worse than a blue alert.'

24 'I toast, therefore I am.'

25 'Let's tool up and go shopping.'

26 'I'm off to see the Wizard.'

27 'It's party time!'

28 'Puncture-repair kit on standby, sir.'

29 'Good crispies, man.'

30 'There's an old human saying, "If you're going to talk
garbage, expect pain."'

31 'I've no fish to embarrass you further; I'll let myself
trout.'

32 'Game over, boys.'

33 'I don't wanna live. Someone, please . . . shoot me in
the head.'

34 'Better dead than smeg.'

35 'Father Christmas, what a bastard.'

36 'I think the android one is punchier.'

37 'Well, this year's calendar would be handy.'

38 'I love this aftershave.'

39 'So what are you going to do? Turn me in, watch me
do the sit-down dance in the electric chair at Sing Sing?'

40 'They're my things, Lister. Would you steal verruca
cream from a man with no feet?'

41 'Perry Como sang "Memories are Made of This" with
one of those stashed in his slacks?'

42 'I'd rather have chicken.'
43 'Don't try to help us; we're finished. Save yourselves.'
44 'Poppycock! It will be happened, it shall be going to be happening, it will be, was an event that could will of been taken place in the future.'
45 'Twice in one lifetime. When you're hot, you're hot.'
46 'Take us to your leader.'

NON-REGISTERED
CREW MEMBERS
Byte 1

Match the guest stars with the characters they played.

1	Lucy Briers	a	Paranoia
2	Simon Gaffney	b	Gelf Bride
3	Mac McDonald	c	Kochanski Camille
4	Maria Friedman	d	Gordon
5	Judy Hawkins	e	Abraham Lincoln
6	Lee Cornes	f	Chen
7	Gordon Salkilld	g	Yvonne McGruder
8	Suzanne Rhatigan	h	Captain Hollister
9	Paul Bradley	i	Harrison
10	Steven Wickham	j	Young Rimmer
11	Jack Klaff	k	Ssertiaw!
12	Charles Augins	l	Commander Binks
13	Matthew Devitt	m	Todhunter
14	Sarah Stockbridge	n	Rimmer's dad
15	Tina Jenkins	o	The Cat Priest
16	Matthew Marsh	p	Queeg
17	John Abineri	q	The Dog
18	Noel Coleman	r	Captain Platini
19	Robert Bathurst	s	The newsreader
20	Don Warrington	t	A handmaiden

WORD SEARCH 1
Happy hour

The words listed on page 19 are 'hidden' in the grid. They may be found written vertically, horizontally or diagonally, and even backwards.

```
L E O P A R D L A G E R Z P V W
B F V W H I Z C L A B E A I I I
X P I E K E E M A N C I E N F C
O B M C Z J C E L O Z R E A A K
C Q T I G D T F I X M R B C O E
N E O U N E H Z Q Y L E M O T D
A I D J L T L J U L E P S L N S
I H O T T O D D I E S V A A G T
B Z T N I A H S D F O M K D C R
O E Y A G U I N N E S S D A T E
N J H R X K U B I L U C O S X N
A M A R G A R I T A Y T V W P G
Z K T U W T O S R J P R E K D T
N G A C E E F F O C U W L V S H
I Q V K S E L N G O E Y B Z G L
C J A C H I C K E N S O U P I A
M S L A N R F P N U T Q O H B G
P F R L V W F X N S H K D Q I E
B M O B A N A N A B D R J M E R
A E Y K S I H W G N I P L U G C
```

BANANA BOMB
BLACKCURRANT JUICE
CHICKEN SOUP
CINZANO BIANCO
COFFEE
DOUBLE VODKA
GUINNESS
GULPING WHISKY
HOT TODDIES
KEEMA
LEOPARD LAGER
LIQUID NITROGEN
MARGARITA
MINT
  JULEPS
NETTLE TEA
PERRIER
PINA COLADAS
SAKE
VIMTO
WICKED-STRENGTH LAGER
WINE

'I'VE NEVER READ . . . A BOOK'

1 Which page in what book did Rimmer 2 keep looking at?
2 Which magazine did Rimmer have piles of?
3 How many pages were there in *Up, Up and Away*?
4 Who wrote *Lolita*?
5 Whose novels did Holly enjoy reading while alone in deep space for three million years?
6 What did Rimmer read in the Escape Pod?
7 How many times did Rimmer read *How to Cope with Your Own Death*?
8 Who was 'The Bible' dedicated to?
9 Who wrote *The Male Eunuch*?
10 Which page did Lister tear out of *Lolita*?
11 What is Rimmer's favourite book?
12 According to Queeg, where did Holly get all his information from?
13 Which book did Rimmer read the night before addressing Z Shift?
14 Who wrote *Learn Japanese*?
15 From which novel had Rimmer's subconscious lifted Tonto Jitterman?
16 In which book did Rimmer hide his diary?
17 Which magazine did Arlene Rimmer read?
18 How many *Zero-Gee Football* magazines did Lister own?

19 In which magazine would you find the article 'Ten
Things You Didn't Know About Gonad Electrocution
Kits'?
20 Which magazine do vultures read?
21 According to Holly, what was the worst book ever
written?
22 Who 'reads' *Tess of the D'Urbervilles*?
23 According to Rimmer's book, how many 'fabulous
chat-up lines' are there?
24 Who reads *Film Fun* magazine?

WORD GRID 1
Insults

Unscramble the words on page 23, which are all favourite insults of the crew of *Red Dwarf*, and then place them horizontally in the grid. If you have placed them in the correct order, the vertical column marked with an arrow will spell out an insult favoured by Holly.

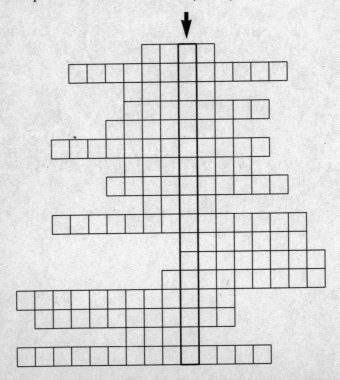

The Questions

BODMIGI
DOOM
FAKEFECRA
GOOFCODEFDA
HOBENDAE
KSEMOROCUSHDEE
KTONW
LAPODIRHDAEO
MECOLLUEDIMN
MSHEAGDE
NWLEYGN
ODRK
OTIG
PALGSHEOODAT
RASHEAREDE
SINOUABRTEDARH
TUGOYR

STAIRCASE 2

When the words listed below are placed horizontally and in the correct order within the grid, they will spell out diagonally (in the boxes marked in bold) another word from *Red Dwarf*.

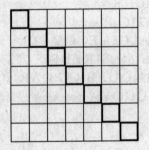

CADMIUM

FLIBBLE

GIMBOID

JUPITER

JUSTICE

MARILYN

SAPIENS

DIETARY REQUIREMENTS

1 What was Josie and Denis's last meal?
2 What was Lister's customary breakfast?
3 What was Rimmer's first meal after three million years?
4 Where did Lister taste his first shami kebab?
5 What did everyone think was the cheese?
6 Who ate banana and crisp sandwiches?
7 What shape was Rimmer's deathday cake?
8 According to Rimmer, what was Todhunter breast-fed on?
9 What does Rimmer attribute his low sex drive to?
10 How many pints was Phil Burroughs's top limit?
11 What sort of biriani has Lister never had?
12 What menu did Kryten plan for Lister after he had seen Lister's future self?
13 Which sort of tea did Juanita prefer?
14 What did Rimmer have for breakfast before he made his voyage to 'Trip-out City'?
15 How many sugars did Henri DuBois take in his coffee?
16 Who offered to be covered in maple syrup?
17 What did Rimmer order in the Last Chance Saloon?
18 What was Lister's last meal before leaving Mimas?
19 How long was Petersen in the medical unit after eating Lister's shami kebab diabolo?
20 What did Lister drink in Euston Road?

21 Who supplied Lister's sausage and onion gravy sandwiches?

22 What did the Cat find in the silver rocks?

23 What tastes like chicken, only two thousand times more expensive?

24 What was Rimmer's last thought?

25 What did Kryten serve to celebrate finding the supergiant?

26 What did Lister get from the vending machine instead of a cup of coffee?

27 What is the 'food of the gods'?

28 What was McIntyre's effigy made of?

29 What vintage champagne does Lister prefer?

30 What sort of vindaloo has Lister never had?

31 What is like a 'cross between food and bowel surgery'?

32 What would Lister rather eat than a pot noodle?

33 Who ate cinema hot dogs?

34 How many tons of mango chutney were retrieved from the *Nova 5*?

35 What was Kryten's 'last meal'?

36 What menu did Rimmer plan for Lister and the Cat that complied with Space Corps requirements?

37 Who is a 'waffle' man?

38 Who used to blow off the bed covers after eating cauliflower cheese?

39 What was Lister's first meal on Garbage World?

40 What type of vindaloo did Lister spill on Rimmer's timetable?

41 When 'shipwrecked and comatose', what would you want to drink?

42 What was Kryten's first meal as a human?

43 Which Rimmer ate mints?

44 What do you have to use to remove a urine re-cyc foam moustache?

45 Where did Lister find the peanuts?

46 How many tons of reconstituted sausage pâté were there on board *Red Dwarf*?

47 What did Lister drink in Whitechapel?

48 How did Rimmer want his whisky before being erased?

49 What did Lister like to start the day with when waking up in the afternoon?

50 What vintage was the Château d'Yquem?

51 According to Holly, what is dog's milk full of?

52 What did Kryten prepare to follow asteroidal lichen stew?

53 Who owned the biggest chain of pizza stores in history?

54 How does Lister like his coffee?

55 How would you eat Mimosian cuisine?

56 Where did Lister get his last meal before joining *Red Dwarf*?

57 Where did Lister get the recipe for his triple fried egg, chilli sauce and chutney sandwich?

58 What did Frankenstein nibble on while her kittens suckled?

59 What was in android home brew?

60 What was Rimmer's favourite pizza?

61 What was Lister's cake supposed to be?

62 What did Lister want with his 'scramble'?

63 Which corridor was out of Crunchie bars?

64 What is Lister's favourite type of sandwich?

65 How many irradiated haggises were there on board
    Red Dwarf?
66 Which company wanted the crew to promote their
    fish fingers?
67 How did Kryten want the chocolate fingers arranged?
68 How many pints of lager does it take Lister to belch
    'La Bamba'?
69 What did Lister keep his chilli sauce in?
70 What did the recycled water begin to taste like?

QUESTIONNAIRE

1) Full name.   Craig Fred Dread Charles

2) Vital statistics.   yes they are arnt they,

3) Height.   not so tall

4) Colour of eyes.   not so Brown

5) Date of birth.   on my birthday

6) Place of birth.   In hospital

7) First job.   being a baby

8) First public
   appearance.   See Question 6

9) First big break.   See Question 6

10) Ambition.   Live Short, Die fast
                              →   Eat Quick (Big family)

11) Hobbies.

12) If you could play any part, which part would you play?
                                  Lister

13) Favourite food/
    drink.   Whisky Tequilla, Crisps

14) Favourite episode of
    Red Dwarf.   Time Slides

15) Least favourite
    episode of Red Dwarf.   The Golden Sausage Cat Prest are

16) Favourite T.V.
    programme(s).   Anything with Bob Llewllyn in

17) Favourite book.   Anything not written by Bob Llewllyn

18) Favourite film.   CLOCKWORK ORANGE

19) Person you most admire, past or present.
                                  Bob Llewellyn

20) Inside leg
    measurement!!!   10 inches

CROSSWORD 2
Lister

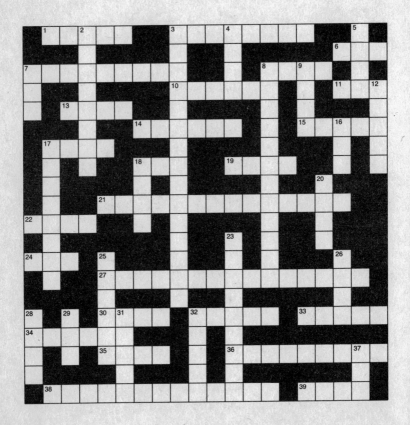

The Questions

Across

1 Lister's Christian name (5)

3 Lister's nickname in Ace's universe (8)

6 Lister earned this on his toast (3)

7 Lister's least favourite food (3,6)

8 Where Lister wanted to buy a farm (4)

10 Lister's musical instrument (6)

11 What Lister was to the Cat people (3)

13 One of Lister's faults is an inclination to be this (4)

14 and 9 down. The Zero–Gee football team Lister supports (6,4)

15 One of Lister's cronies (5)

17 The game Lister played with planets (4)

18 Lister has more of this than a Turkish butcher (3)

19 One of Lister's group (4)

21 Lister's hero (3,6,5)

22 The Aigburth . . . . is where Lister played pool (4)

24 Lister's female equivalent (3)

27 Lister's rank (5,10)

30 A drink favoured by 'old' Lister (4)

32 See 7 down

33 . . . . . Hilton Blanket (5)

34 A space . . . . . . is eaten by Lister (6)

35 See 28 down

36 and 12 down. Lister's alter ego (9,5)

38 *It's a* . . . . is Lister's favourite film (9,4)

39 . . . . glam – a type of music played by Lister (4)

Down

2 A type of curry (8)

3 The band Lister used to belong to (4,3,3,5)

4 Lister certainly isn't this! (4)

5 and 29. The type of football Lister is a fan of (4,3)

7 and 32 across. Monopoly board . . . . (3,5)

8 The name of Lister's pet cat (12)

9 See 14 across

12 See 36 across

16 Lister taught Kryten how to do this (3)

17 Lister's best mate (8)

18 and 20. What Lister became while in Better Than Life (4,4)

20 See 18 down

23 The love of Lister's life (9)

25 Lister spent three million years in this state (6)

26 Lister is the . . . . human alive (4)

28 and 35 across. Lister's offspring (4,4)

29 See 5 down

31 '. . . . . in a godless universe' (5)

32 Lister used to catch condoms in this (5)

37 Lister as an old man has a robotic one of these (3)

NON-REGISTERED CREW MEMBERS
Byte 2

Match the guest stars with the characters they played.

1	Tony Hawks	a	Simulant Lieutenant
2	Emille Charles	b	Simulant
3	Martin Friend	c	Lise Yates
4	Denis Lill	d	The cop
5	Morwenna Banks	e	Android actor
6	Timothy Spall	f	Hector Blob
7	Kalli Greenwood	g	Kryten
8	Liz Hickling	h	Simulant Captain
9	Nicholas Ball	i	Einstein
10	Sabra Williams	j	Young Lister
11	Jenny Agutter	k	Rimmer's mum
12	Judy Pascoe	l	Marilyn Monroe
13	Stephen Marcus	m	Miss Lola
14	Rupert Bates	n	Lift hostess
15	Lenny Von Dohlen	o	Mechanoid Camille
16	Imogen Bain	p	Caligula
17	Debbie Ash	q	Andy
18	Sophie Doherty	r	Bear Strangler McGee
19	David Ross	s	Professor Mamet
20	Tony Slattery	t	Kochanski's room-mate

JIG WORD 1

Take the words from the columns on page 35 and fit them into the grid wherever space (and sense!) allows, so that they form a crossword.

The Questions

3 Letters

ACE
DNA
GOD
INN

4 Letters

ACID
DATE
DAVE
JAKE
LEGO
TIME
VAIN

5 Letters

ANGER
GUILT
SPACE
STYLE

6 Letters

BULLET
GELDOF
KIPPER
MONKEY
OILING
SATURN
STASIS

7 Letters

AMATEUR
ANDROID
GINGHAM
GRAVITY
SAPIENS

8 Letters

INFINITE
SAUSAGES
UNIVERSE

DEEP SMEG!
Megabyte 1

So 'Smeg!' left you in 'smug mode', did it? Well, try these for size!

1 How many floors of food were there aboard *Red Dwarf*?
2 What did the 'Blue Hats' believe Lister's laundry list was?
3 How long had Rimmer known Porky Roebuck?
4 Whose sinal fluid did Rimmer give Kryten?
5 How many and what sex were the crew of the *Nova 5*?
6 What was the Cat's 'sacred icon' really?
7 How many minutes does it take until the Inquisitor 'unfreezes'?
8 For how many years was Rimmer imprisoned by his clones?
9 How long did it take Lister and Rimmer to get to the top of the Cat's island?
10 Where did Frankenstein come from?
11 What does '*Mi esporas ke kiam vi venos la vetero estos milda*' mean?
12 What would the Cat rather do than wear grey out of season?
13 Who said, 'Shiny clean boots and a spanking short haircut, and you can cope with anything'?
14 Who climbed out of a toilet window?

15 Which station follows Oxford Street in Monopoly?

16 Who was King of Crap?

17 How many times did *Red Dwarf* fly around 'Felicity Kendal's bottom'?

18 According to his tattoo, who does Lister really love?

19 What did Lister steal from Rimmer's study?

20 What did Lister erase from Holly's memory banks?

21 What is Lister's second worst fear?

22 What does 'KIT' stand for?

23 When should Rimmer use his Chinese worry balls?

24 Who has green urine?

25 What did Rimmer want to clone himself with when using the DNA Modifier?

26 What is the number of the Hologram Suite?

27 In which two episodes does the Cat 'make himself look big'?

28 How much was Petersen's house, and how many bedrooms did it have?

29 What was the cause of the Cat Wars?

30 Who was ninety-eight when he died?

31 Who had to organize his own surprise birthday parties?

32 How tall was Frank Rimmer at the age of eleven?

33 What was Kristine Kochanski's rank?

34 Where did Lister earn the name of 'Cinzano Bianco', and why?

35 How many seconds did Rimmer give the captain to come back from the dead?

36 Name the Gelf Tribe.

37 What was Lister's single most important piece of advice to himself?

38 How old will Rimmer really be when his body is seventy-eight?

39 What religion were Rimmer's parents?

40 Where had Kryten seen more convincing dinosaurs?

41 On which corridor did Lister faint?

42 What was the make of Rimmer's caffeine tablets?

43 On which deck is Parrot's Bar?

44 What was the *Enlightenment*'s computer called?

45 Who did Rimmer say Kryten and Lister were chained together like?

46 What is the Female Simulant doing tonight?

47 Who stole Rimmer's body?

48 Who probably has more teeth than brain cells?

49 How long did the Cat Wars last?

50 What did Lister use as a fridge?

51 How many times did Rimmer object to his own defence?

52 What does 'AR' stand for?

53 How many members were there in Z Shift?

54 What was the 'Ultimate Machine'?

55 How many complaints did Rimmer file against Lister?

56 Who did the Blu-Tak belong to?

57 What did Rimmer call Lister, the Cat and Kryten after six hundred years?

58 What was the rendezvous point after going round the black holes?

59 Where was the Agoraphobic Society AGM held?

60 What time was Kryten's driving test?

61 Who did Lister first bodyswap with?

62 Why did Kryten believe that Lister was a droid?

63 What was the colour of the carpet in the Rimmer Building lobby?

64 How long does the average Mimian traffic jam last?

65 Who's a 'little lamb who's lost in the woods'?

66 At what age was Self-Confidence taken?

67 With the aid of the triplicator, how long will it take to make a full fruit salad?

68 How many cats were there when Frankenstein died?

69 How often did Rimmer have access to the family dog?

70 According to Rimmer, where do you settle for if you can't have two weeks in the Caribbean?

71 Other than Lister, who didn't read any books?

72 At what time was troop inspection?

73 Where was Sebastian Doyle's limo parked?

74 Who did Lister think the Cat might have bought his island from?

75 On how many doors was Kryten used as a battering ram?

76 What happened to people who didn't eat hot dogs on Fuchal Day?

77 Whom did Rimmer hope the aliens wouldn't return?

78 Who was Jimmy's brother?

79 What did Lister swap Rimmer's toothpaste for?

80 When would Kryten's shut-down disk be operated?

81 Which decision would Rimmer regret for ever?

82 What is better than listening to an album by Olivia Newton-John?

83 Which cuisine is acceptable to mechanoids?

84 How long were Lister and Cat in 'prolonged deep sleep'?

85 Where is the Quarantine Room?

86 Who went into Better Than Life second?

87 Who owns the Saturnian satellite of Mimas?

88 Who was being 'thicker than the offspring of a village idiot and a TV weathergirl'?

89 Who was the Inquisitor's first victim?

90 What is the fifth dimension?

91 Who was Hannah?

92 How long did it take Lister to wear out the groinal attachment on the AR Machine?

93 What colour was Lister's exit sign?

94 What did Rimmer's brothers hide in his sandpit?

95 What was Rimmer going to get Dr Lanstrom for Christmas?

96 How did Frank Saunders die?

97 Why did Rimmer's body need to be oiled?

98 What does Kryten's right nipple do?

99 What year was Captain Hollister 'Mr Fat Bastard'?

100 How many times had Rimmer failed the entrance exam for the Academy?

101 What will happen if the O/G Unit doesn't work?

102 What does Rimmer hate more than anything?

103 Why did Rimmer 'wear' two pairs of socks?

104 How many years' penal servitude should Rimmer have served?

105 What waiting list did Lister put Rimmer's name on?

106 How did the new Rimmarian calendar run?

107 What was Lister's group motto?

108 Due to a programming error, where did the Teleporter take the crew?

109 What is the speed limit for the universe?

110 Which episodes feature the Matter Paddle?

111 What was the turning point in Cat history?

112 How much was the divorce settlement that Rimmer paid Juanita?

113 Who was the ship's psychiatrist?

114 How many pelvic thrusts per second can an Iranian Jerd do?

115 How old was Frankenstein when she died?

116 Who said, 'Never give a sucker an even break'?

117 How much Outland Revenue tax did Rimmer owe?

118 Who was called a 'munchkin'?

119 According to Rimmer, what is death really like?

120 How did the Cats learn English?

121 Who used to be 'faster than a toilet stop in rattlesnake country'?

122 How far away was the nearest thorium-bearing moon?

123 What was Mother Theresa's rank?

124 What does Lister make his guitar 'sing' like?

125 Apart from breathe, what can't you do in a methane atmosphere?

126 Which Wednesday after Pentecost is referred to?

127 Who filled in the 'Have You Got a Good Memory' quiz?

128 How many years has Lister eaten curries non-stop?

WORD SEARCH 2
Baddies!

The words listed opposite are 'hidden' in the grid. They may be found written vertically, horizontally or diagonally, and even backwards.

```
A C Z N T H O Y W M O N S T E R
S U M R F L I B B L E J M H P P
M R X E N B D T F R C P H E A H
E R E N O P A C L A O G M A D Z
N Y C G W C O M Q E W O R P G B
O L P S I R E N S D R S I O I D
E M O H A W K D Z T S N G C S I
L H L E D N T H S T I L N A O U
B Q Y V U C S N N L B D E L A Q
A C M Y K E A A O E I X T Y J S
K T O M P L L S U H R V N P F R
A I R J R U S F N P O I E S U I
E L P D M U E A Z K T N Z E I A
P T H I M R M G S U I K D B T P
S E S L I X A J P B S R U O G S
N R H K A Q J S Q C I A H Y J E
U V F T M H A B A D U Y F S P D
E A E O X R F V S W Q U E E G E
H H Q E C N E D I F N O C R T H
T H E H O L Y L E G I O N S W T
```

The Questions

AL CAPONE
THE APOCALYPSE BOYS
CONFIDENCE
CURRY
MONSTER
THE DESPAIR SQUID
DR LANSTROM
EMOHAWK
HITLER
THE HOLY LEGIONS
HUDZEN TEN
INQUISITOR
JAMES LAST
MR FLIBBLE
MUSSOLINI
POLYMORPH
PSIRENS
QUEEG
RASPUTIN
SIMULANTS
THE TAXMAN
THE UNSPEAKABLE ONE

CLOTHES

(or distraction from the pursuit of intellectual fulfilment)

1 What colour were Rimmer's swimming goggles?

2 How many suits could the Cat take into stasis?

3 What colour were Lister's lucky underpants originally?

4 For how long had Kryten been scrubbing the gussets on Lister's long johns?

5 Who wore 'smart shoes'?

6 What was it necessary to wear when Sunday dinner was being served at the Rimmers' house?

7 Where can Hugo no longer buy shoes?

8 Who does Lister claim wears 'extra brown-rubber safety pants'?

9 What colour tie was Jim Bexley Speed wearing when interviewed after Megabowl 102?

10 Who wore an orange and black baseball cap?

11 What costume did Lister like to wear when making love?

12 Who wore sturdy, sensible underpants?

13 What smells like 'an orang-utan's posing pouch'?

14 What colour was the jumper returned by Kochanski?

15 What would the Cat rather do than wear suits with arrows on?

16 Who created 'that outfit'?

17 Where were Lister's moon boots kept?

18 What colour was Rimmer's ski jacket?

19 In which episodes does Rimmer wear a white officer's uniform?
20 Who wore Goofy slippers?
21 Which T-shirt does Lister only wear on special occasions?
22 According to his quiz, what does Lister wear when alone in bed?
23 Who wears jet-powered rocket pants?
24 How long does Lister extend the wear time of his underpants by turning them inside out?

WHO SAID THIS, AND WHERE?
Byte 2

State the characters in *Red Dwarf* who said the following, and in which episodes.

1 'Oh smeg indeed, matey.'
2 'If God had intended us to fly, he wouldn't have invented Spanish air traffic control.'
3 'The only way we're going to track down *Red Dwarf* and get through this in one piece is with a sense of discipline, a sense of purpose and wherever possible a sensible haircut.'
4 'Say hello, then, won't you. Only trying to be friendly.'
5 'Whose head's that, then?'
6 'You call that dancing. I've seen people on fire move better than that.'
7 'Well, darling, I'm pooped. Straight to sleep for me.'
8 'You goit. No, you goit. You're all goits. I'm surrounded by goits.'
9 'I think you're perfectly charming.'
10 'Let's do lunch sometime. I'll put it in my diary. 12.30: Lunch with God.'
11 'We're going to die.'
12 'Now you've got it in stereo, baby.'
13 'What happened to my butt, buddy? You could park a plane in that crease.'

14 'I wish I'd never let him out in the first place now.'

15 'Sir, you are a cruddy little scudball, with all the innate lovability of an itchy verruca.'

16 'Right, if we can just teach her to count without banging her head on the screen, it's going to be an improvement.'

17 'You're a filthy, smegging, lying, smegging liar.'

18 'Cat, you're so gullible.'

19 'Yes, Mum, I'm just packing my satchel.'

20 'Guess what: I lied.'

21 'Oh, for a really world-class psychiatrist.'

22 'I've got a window in my schedule this afternoon.'

23 'Mind that bus! What bus? Splat!'

24 'Flats or heels?'

25 'Erm, Hercule Poirot's just stepped off the steaming train. If you want my opinion, I think they all did it.'

26 'No plan, sir, no sleeves.'

27 'I think I'm going to do something secret.'

28 'Damn you both, all the way to Hades. I want to go to blue alert.'

29 'Look out, Earth, the slime's coming home.'

30 'This guy's an animal. Doesn't he know it's red wine with cold ashes.'

31 'I think I've just worked out what that missing circuit board was for, sir.'

32 'Nice idea, goal-post head.'

33 'See Dick run, run Dick run, run home, Dick.'

34 'Kryten. Kryten. There may be what? A way out of this? Is that what you were going to say? Speak, Kryten; how can we change what's happening?'

35 'It took me ages to mark these cards.'

36 'Oh, gimme a break.'

37 'Arnold, where are the nappy sacks?'

38 'Have you quite finished being strange?'

39 'My God. I was only away two minutes.'

40 'Carol: next corpse, please.'

41 'Rimmer? He's my best mate, isn't he?'

42 'Yeah, we're cooking now.'

43 'Watch my dreams.'

44 'And the things this boy can do with alphabetti spaghetti.'

45 'What's the beef? Did she steal your lunchbox?'

STAIRCASE 3

When the words listed below are placed horizontally and in the correct order within the grid, they will spell out diagonally (in the boxes marked in bold) another word from *Red Dwarf*.

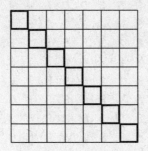

DIARIES
HERRING
MIRRORS
PLATINI
POLLOCK
REALITY
SAPIENS

NUMBER SEARCH

The answers to questions 1–32 are 'hidden' in the grid below. They may be found arranged vertically, horizontally, diagonally, and even backwards.

```
3 6 0 0 4 9 4 X 4 R E 1 3 D W 2
9 9 4 1 3 5 3 0 0 6 4 4 2 X 9 0
1 5 9 2 9 N 4 9 1 9 6 4 B 0 2 2
X 0 0 1 8 2 3 5 5 4 1 F 4 1 6 0
4 1 7 2 X 0 Z 4 1 6 7 3 2 W 4 7
B 9 1 7 9 1 2 6 5 B 9 6 9 5 1 7
2 4 7 V 5 4 F 0 8 3 5 0 2 6 8 0
Z X 1 8 8 0 0 0 3 P 4 3 0 E C 2
i 3 E 5 6 8 9 3 W 6 0 0 0 0 5 3
B 0 3 4 7 A 4 1 5 C 9 4 0 A 0 2
4 B B 0 5 3 Z 5 4 4 6 2 8 5 0 6
X 5 4 E 9 4 8 2 8 7 4 0 6 1 B 1
2 4 2 0 3 5 B 8 6 9 5 0 X 3 B 6
W 6 7 9 X 7 5 1 5 7 0 7 0 9 2 4
7 i T G 0 0 0 4 9 0 4 5 8 2 3 9
4 7 A 7 9 3 1 0 9 X 5 4 6 8 9 7
3 4 4 5 3 4 0 0 9 2 6 N 4 1 3 0
2 8 1 2 X 2 Y 0 6 0 7 9 8 8 Z 2
5 7 6 4 0 3 1 0 5 4 0 X 9 C 2 6
9 6 1 0 0 0 6 i W 4 Z 1 3 4 5 1
```

1 Lister's security code
2 Machine code for 'love'
3 The number of years of penal servitude for Rimmer
4 The number of the android in the bus queue
5 The quantity of rehydrated chickens
6 Camille's series number
7 *Red Dwarf*'s postal code
8 Gordon's IQ
9 Kryten's middle 'name'
10 The number of *Friday the Thirteenths*
11 Holly's IQ
12 The year it was on Backwards World
13 The sector where the *Enlightenment* was found
14 The age at which Lister lost his virginity
15 The number of Holly's first love
16 The number of the Honeymoon Suite at the Ganymede Holiday Inn
17 The year Captain Hollister was Mr Fat Bastard
18 The total number of episodes of *Red Dwarf* to date
19 The series number of Kelly in *Androids*
20 Nirvanah Crane's crew number
21 The day of the month for Gazpacho Soup Day
22 Hercule Platini's IQ
23 The level of *Red Dwarf* on which the Cat first appeared
24 'Groovy' Channel
25 The number of the Quarantine Room
26 The quantity of irradiated haggises
27 The Hologram Projection Suite is on this level
28 The date on which stasis leaked
29 The bay where Sebastian Doyle parked his car

30 The series number of Brooke Junior
31 Natalina Pushkin's IQ
32 The number of complaints Rimmer had against Lister

SPACE CORPS DIRECTIVES

How well do you know your Space Corps Directives? Get out your manual and start studying *now*; then see how many of the following Directives you can remember.

1 Article 497 of the Space Corps Directive?
2 Space Corps Directive No. 1743?
3 Space Corps Directive No. 699?
4 Rimmer Directive No. 271?
5 According to Kryten, which Space Corps Directive is impossible without at least one live chicken and a rabbi?
6 Space Corps Directive No. 34124?
7 Space Corps Directive No. 1742?
8 Article 5 of the Space Corps Directive?
9 Space Corps Directive No. 312?
10 Space Corps Directive No. 196156?
11 Space Corps Directive No. 597?
12 Space Corps Directive No. 39436175880932/B?

JIG WORD 2

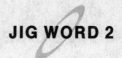

Take the words from the columns opposite and fit them into the grid wherever space (and sense!) allows, so that they form a crossword.

3 Letters

ARN
DNA
HEX
HOP
LIE
PSI

4 Letters

CHEN
FIJI
POOL

5 Letters

DUANE
DWARF
JUDAS
LUNAR
SPACE
WILMA

6 Letters

ANORAK
ARNOLD
AWOOGA
BANANA
LUPINO
NELLIE
NODNOL
NORWEB
PLANET
POPEYE

7 Letters

CAPTAIN
SKIPPER

8 Letters

APPENDIX
COMPUTER
LANSTROM
NAPOLEON

DEEP SMEG!
Megabyte 2

So 'Deep smeg! – Megabyte 1' wasn't enough for you?
You want more? OK then, but remember: you are *not* a
fish!

1 When did Rimmer make a journey to 'Trip-out
    City'?
2 Who was 'The Despicable One'?
3 Which century would Rimmer choose if he could be
    anywhere in time?
4 How many days did Rimmer save in stasis?
5 Who invented unicycle polo?
6 On how many counts of murder was Rimmer found
    guilty?
7 How long is it until 'El Skutto' has to be back on
    duty?
8 What time was it when Rimmer stood in the main
    washroom and combed his hair?
9 What characteristics are missing from Duane?
10 What colour did Rimmer order the skutters to change
    the ocean grey to?
11 What did the black card signify?
12 What is the connection between Kryten and Talkie
    Toaster?
13 Which two 'groups' had a hit with 'Baby I Want Your
    Love Thing', and what number did they get to?

14 How did Legion snare *Starbug*?

15 Which hole was Lister on when he lost his virginity and what par was it?

16 What minimum leisure facilities did Rimmer provide for Lister, the Cat and Kryten while they were in quarantine?

17 Who was the coffee lounge named after in the Mimas Hilton?

18 Who was 'El Weirdo'?

19 Who was Kryten's creator?

20 How did the Polymorph escape *Blue Midget*?

21 From whom was Lister the only man ever to get his money back?

22 How much were Juanita's breasts insured for?

23 How much weight did Lister gain when Rimmer 'borrowed' his body?

24 Where was Alexander the Great's palace?

25 How many days did it take Kryten and Rimmer to get to and from the cargo decks?

26 Which planet has a methane atmosphere?

27 Who was no longer a threat to the crew's marriages?

28 Who despised idiots and had no time for fools?

29 Where did Petersen buy the Marilyn Monroe droid kit?

30 What are the luxury extras on a GTi?

31 Whose bottom was put with whose boobs?

32 What does a Dove Program do?

33 How many per cent did the crew score in 'Red Dwarf'?

34 What was Rimmer's team chant?

35 Why did Rimmer have Petersen's arm?

36 Who looked 'absolutely perfect'?

37 What is wrong with Lister's Monopoly board?

38 How long was Lister waiting to be rescued from Garbage World?

39 What would Lister rather do than spend fifty years alone with Rimmer?

40 How much was Rimmer once offered for General George S. Patton's sinal fluid?

41 What are the two types from Assisi?

42 How many men had Loretta killed?

43 Who was a millionaire at twenty-six?

44 What did Trixie LaBouche's tattoo read?

45 Whose dad did the Purley Bank Job?

46 What did Rimmer lose when he was twelve?

47 What did Rimmer buy Juanita as a 'kiss-and-make-up gift'?

48 What human qualities does Kryten admire most?

49 What was the number of the wormhole that the escape pod took Rimmer through?

50 What did Josie have a degree in?

51 Why did Lister think that he had once 'sold out'?

52 What was tattooed on Petersen's arm?

53 What was the most romantic thing that Rimmer had ever had in his ear?

54 When will the car stickers be ready?

55 How many condoms did Saunders leave in his bedside cabinet, and what flavour were they?

56 Where did Lister go on his school camping trip?

57 What did Kryten's friend Gilbert like to be called?

58 What is the difference between an android and a simulant?

59 How many people lived in Bedford Falls?

60 What was considered the height of bad manners aboard the *Enlightenment*?

61 Who was trapped in the lair of the 'surfboarding killer bikini vampire girls'?

62 What APR did the Ganymedian Mafia charge?

63 What does Rimmer believe in instead of God?

64 What rank did Rimmer's mother think he was?

65 What did Rimmer do on Day One upon landing on Rimmerworld?

66 Which planet was in Universe 3?

67 What was the level of gravity at the Titan Taj Mahal?

68 How much money had Rimmer managed to scrimp and scrape together?

69 Whose 'tits' (or nipples) did Lister threaten to rip off?

70 What was Lister's party piece?

71 How big was the meteor that came towards *Starbug* just before the crew encountered the Psirens?

72 What star signs were Denis and Josie?

73 What did Rimmer do when he was fourteen?

74 What follows the leaflet campaign?

75 What does Kryten have in common with Action Man?

76 Where did McIntyre play Toot?

77 On what did Lister make his Chef's exam notes?

78 According to Lister, when is the party over?

79 How long is the waiting list for 'Red Dwarf'?

80 Who ate his wife?

81 In whose nose did Lister shelter?

82 Who is described as 'a couple of gunmen short of a posse'?

83 At what time did the cadmium 2 core reach critical mass?

84 What was the only direction the crew's future selves could travel in?

85 Where did Rimmer hide Lister's cigarettes?

86 When is Lister's birthday?

87 What did Rimmer believe the 'Quagaars' had the technology to do?

88 What was the supply situation after two hundred years?

89 Where did the 'attack of the killer gooseberries' take place?

90 How many months'/years' wages did Lister lose in stasis?

91 What was Rimmer's code name during the Wax War?

92 Who was the leader of A Shift?

93 Who did Rimmer join for port and cigars?

94 How many years did Lister spend as a Trolley Assistant?

95 Where was Holly going to hang Queeg?

96 Who was Phil Burroughs?

97 Where did Josie buy her headset?

98 If mechanoids could 'barf', which bag would Kryten be into?

99 What was Legion's 'psycho rating'?

100 What was Sammy the Squib's preferred weapon?

101 Which floor is referred to for a 'quick chukka'?

102 What was Z Shift's most important duty?

103 What sort of deodorant does Lister use?

104 Who didn't think that men were better than machines?

105 How long did it take Lister to save $£53?

106 Who had oiled nipples (other than Rimmer!)?

107 What did Rimmer have to do 'because he's so wet'?

108 What did Rimmer launch when first on Rimmerworld?

109 Who blessed Lister's cue?

110 Why couldn't Rimmer's dad join the Space Corps?

111 How many times did Lister make love to 'Rimmer's mum'?

112 Which moon rotates in the opposite direction to the planet it is orbiting?

113 How much did Frankenstein cost?

114 Who did Rimmer beat at Risk when he was seventeen?

115 What were Rimmer's criteria for choosing who was to use the escape pod?

116 What did the Cat ask Lister to do to prove that he was God?

117 Who said, 'Never apologize, never explain'?

118 Who did the crew's future selves play canasta with?

119 Where did Lister get the 'freaky fungus' from?

120 How did Rimmer and Lister get to the top of the Cat's island?

121 What is considered normal behaviour on Rimmerworld?

122 What did Lister state as his occupation when on the witness stand?

123 Who 'bagsied' Rimmer's right buttock?

124 Which planet is 'nearer than you think'?

125 How many times had it been Christmas Eve in Bedford Falls?

126 How many minutes did Lister give the crew's future selves to get off of *Starbug*?

127 What makes Lister 'prunable'?

128 What sort of woman did Rimmer believe was inside the 'alien' capsule?

129 What is termed a 'short-term hormonal distraction which interferes with the pure pursuit of personal advancement'?

130 What was Rimmer going to get the skutters to paint on a plaque?

131 Who invented the 'condom that calls you back'?

BACK-ROOM BOYS AND GIRLS

1 Who directed Series I and II?
2 Which episodes did Rob Grant and Doug Naylor solely direct?
3 Who took over Make-up Design from Suzanne Jansen?
4 Who wrote the *Red Dwarf* theme tune?
5 In which episode was Colin Skeaping a stuntman?
6 Who produced Series V?
7 Who took over as Costume Designer from Jackie Pinks?
8 Which episode did Rocket first work on?
9 Name the Visual Effects Designer.
10 Who provided the disco music for 'Balance of Power'?
11 Who choreographed 'Tongue Tied' in 'Parallel Universe'?
12 Who was the SSS *Esperanto* Director?
13 Who was Videotape Editor for Series I, II and III?
14 Who preceded Mel Bibby as Designer?
15 For which episode in Series III was Keith Mayes the Sound Supervisor?
16 Who was Executive Producer for Series I, II and III?
17 Who directed Series VI?
18 Which two episodes has Nick Kool worked on?
19 What role has John Pomphrey had in every series?
20 Who took over from Ed Wooden as Videotape Editor?

21 For which episodes in Series I was Duncan Wheeler *not* Properties Buyer?

22 Who was Vision Mixer for Series I and II?

23 Who was the OB Cameraman on 'Backwards', 'Marooned' and 'Timeslides'?

24 Name the Stage Manager for Series IV and V.

25 Who was in charge of video effects for Series VI?

26 What was Mark Allen's role in Series I, II and III?

27 Who was Unit Manager for Series I?

28 For which episode in Series V was Peter Bates the Insert Editor?

29 Who was Location Manager for 'Emohawk – Polymorph II'?

30 What was the role of Gerard Naprous in 'Gunmen of the Apocalypse'?

STAIRCASE 4

When the words listed below are placed horizontally and in the correct order within the grid, they will spell out diagonally (in the boxes marked in bold) another word from *Red Dwarf*.

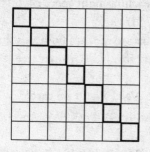

CAMILLE
CAPTAIN
GARBAGE
JUPITER
MIRANDA
MONKEYS
PORKMAN

'CAN YOU SEE THAT SPACE VEHICLE?'

1 What was the *Nova 5*'s original mission?
2 What is the registration of *Starbug*?
3 What was the name of the ship that brought Petersen to Mimas?
4 How many years does it take for *Red Dwarf* to turn around after reaching light speed?
5 How big is *Red Dwarf*?
6 What was the name of Captain Tau's ship?
7 What craft did Howard Rimmer test at Houston?
8 Where did the *Nova 5* land on earth?
9 What is *Starbug* in comparison to a Class D Space Corps seeding ship?
10 In which area of space was the *Enlightenment* discovered?
11 How many gears does *Blue Midget* have?
12 What has *Starbug* crashed more times than?
13 Where was the Space Corps test base?
14 What is the cruising speed of *Red Dwarf*?
15 What was the supply ship called?
16 Using the Star Drive, how long should it have taken *Starbug* to catch up with *Red Dwarf*?
17 What was the SSS *Esperanto*'s mission?
18 Which flight boarded at Gate 5?
19 What was the *Nova 5* made of?

20 Which pilot seat didn't go up and down after the flaming meteor hit *Starbug*?
21 What is the stopping distance for half the speed of light?
22 How much did a shuttle ticket from Mimas to Earth cost?
23 What did Kryten go in search of on Lister's space bike?

WORD SEARCH 3
Cosmic!

The words listed opposite are 'hidden' in the grid. They may be found written vertically, horizontally or diagonally, and even backwards.

```
C O S U N A R U A I S E S N T T
M A B O K Y O A R S S R E V O I
T R L T A N R H E O D R A O E T
S M I L K Y W A Y M E Y H M D A
C I S T I O M A S R H O O T U N
N L V E U S A N K U M R D U P O
O N E P A G T O J L U E A R T H
O M I T E A N O T I R T U R I S
M E U S P O A X B E A I N O O T
V R O L T L E N O O C P A L L A
N U E S K A U I T A N U S I U E
C A L M O U R T G N O J A N I A
E N U T P E N V O Q U O C O Y E
A S T E I H T P S U E N S R U D
U S O L L A O R O X K O U K P E
S O M U T U S E V A R C N I A M
A R H E U C R T B O R A E C S Y
M D E Q F H E O S E Y N V E O N
I O V L E A P S M Q U E F U S A
M I R A N D A D O O C U L T O G
```

CALLISTO
EARTH
GANYMEDE
IO
JUPITER
MARS
MERCURY
MILKY WAY
MIMAS
MIRANDA
MOON
NEPTUNE
PHOEBE
PLUTO
RHEA
SATURN
SUN
TITAN
TRITON
URANUS
VENUS

NON-REGISTERED
CREW MEMBERS
Byte 3

Match the guest stars with the characters they played.

1	Robert Addie	a	Deb Lister
2	Francesca Follan	b	Marilyn Monroe
3	Francine Walker-Lee	c	Confidence
4	Johanna Hargreaves	d	Elvis Presley
5	Stephen Tiller	e	Talkie Toaster (Series I)
6	Nigel Williams	f	Nirvanah Crane
7	Angela Bruce	g	American TV presenter
8	Craig Ferguson	h	New Lister ('Back to
9	Ron Pember		Reality')
10	Pauline Bailey	i	Pythagoras
11	Maggie Steed	j	Hologram Camille
12	Anita Dobson	k	Arlene Rimmer
13	John Sharian	l	Genny Mutant
14	John Lenahan	m	Gilbert
15	Suzanne Bertish	n	Stan Laurel
16	Frances Barber	o	Dr Lanstrom
17	Ruby Wax	p	The Taxman
18	Forbes Masson	q	A handmaiden
19	Jane Horrocks	r	Legion
20	Clayton Mark	s	Esperanto teacher
		t	Captain Tau

QUESTIONNAIRE

1) Full name. Norman Lovett

2) Vital statistics. How dare you!

3) Height. 5'10"

4) Colour of eyes. Blue

5) Date of birth. 31-10-46

6) Place of birth. Windsor

7) First job. Clerk

8) First public appearance. Pub in Kings Road Chelsea (Wheatsheaf).

9) First big break. Still waiting.

10) Ambition. To keep working.

11) Hobbies. My family, my work and eating walnuts.

12) If you could play any part, which part would you choose?

I can't think of anything at this moment.

13) Favourite food/ drink. Squid with black bean sauce. Wine.

14) Favourite episode of Red Dwarf. Queeg & Kryten Series II

15) Least favourite episode of Red Dwarf. I refuse to answer this.

16) Favourite T.V. programme(s). 'If you see God Tell Him' BBC1

17) Favourite book. Animal Farm

18) Favourite film. Duel (Spielberg).

19) Person you most admire, past or present. My wife Fiona.

20) Inside leg measurement!!! 31"

CROSSWORD 3
Holly

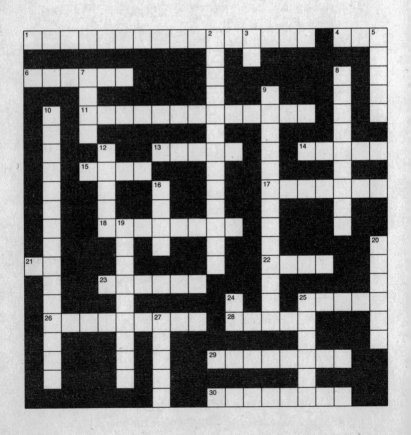

The Questions

Across

1 What Holly suffers from (8,8)
4 The initials of the company that owns *Red Dwarf* (3)
6 Holly's postal chess partner (6)
11 Holly's farewell song (7,2,4)
13 The docking port where Holly was going to hang Queeg (5)
14 Holly's 'parallel' equal (5)
15 The only part of Holly you ever see (4)
17 Holly's decimalized music (3,4)
18 It can't cope with the influx of data at light speed (8)
21 Unidentified Object (2)
22 Holly suffered from a computer one of these when he met Hilly (4)
23 Holly wore one of these when *Blue Midget* found the *Nova 5* (6)
25 Holly was this for 3 million years (5)
26 Holly has plenty of these (9)
28 Holly? (5)
29 See 25 down
30 Holly's first love was one of these (8)

Down

2 Holly was reduced to this occupation when Queeg took over (5,8)
3 Light Speed (2)
5 The type of contest Holly undertook with Queeg (5)
7 Plenty of this sort of milk was left on board (4)
8 '. . . . ., May, June, July, August, ...' (5,4)

9 How to 'parallel universe' jump (5,3,5)
10 Holly's collection of these helped keep him sane (7,8)
12 Holly's 'number' blind spot (5)
16 What the black holes turned out to be (4)
19 It's 'muggins' really! (9)
20 You'll see Holly's face on one of these (6)
24 Holly's is six thousand (2)
25 and 29 across. The novelist whose books were all erased from Holly's memory banks (6,8)
27 Blue, purple or red . . . . . (5)

QUESTIONNAIRE

1) Full name. HATTIE HAYRIDGE

2) Vital statistics. Size 6½ stiletto

3) Height. 6ft 2" in above

4) Colour of eyes. Blue and blue

5) Date of birth. Too young to remember at the time

6) Place of birth. Was Middx now London

7) First job. Saturday job in Sketchley's

8) First public appearance. A red ant in the school play

9) First big break. 'See above'

10) Ambition. To have a picture of me eating a pickled onion in front of Sunday supplements.

11) Hobbies. Air traffic controlling

12) If you could play any part, which part would you play? The dark haired one in Gentlemen Prefer Blondes

13) Favourite food/drink. Custard

14) Favourite episode of Red Dwarf. All of them

15) Least favourite episode of Red Dwarf. There isn't one

16) Favourite T.V. programme(s). What else?

17) Favourite book. World Atlas

18) Favourite film. Life of Brian

19) Person you most admire, past or present. Arnold Rimmer

20) Inside leg measurement!!! I'll ask when I next go to Burtons

WORD GRID 2
Space sickness

Unscramble the words listed opposite, which are all medical conditions that have affected characters in *Red Dwarf*, and then place them horizontally in the grid. If you have placed them in the correct order, the vertical column marked with an arrow will spell out an affliction one of the crew is particularly prone to.

The Questions

CAGREPNYN
ETADH
FUDNDAFR
KOBNLERGSE
LOVUSOHRI
MILERUDI
PCSMAMUSPE
PUCORSITEYILTNEM
RAIDEOHAR
SPOCUHARETMR
TIOGIDESNIN
TRIRDOOD

OH SMEG INDEED, MATEY!
Megabyte 1

Do you speak Japanese, Mandarin or Satsuma? If so, you won't need a mind patch to answer these.

1 How much energy per second does it take to sustain a hologramatic simulation of a full human personality?
2 Who did Lister wipe off on to his jacket cuff?
3 How many words did Lister ever exchange with Kochanski?
4 Which exam should Rimmer have been taking when he went swimming by mistake?
5 What attachments can Kryten plug into his groinal socket?
6 How many inoculations did Lister have on joining *Red Dwarf*?
7 Where was the Cat going to leave his body to?
8 Who were to continue painting the Engineers' Mess?
9 What was the new record time for 'scrambling in a red alert situation'?
10 How many skutters had exploded after three weeks spent restoring the *Nova 5*?
11 Where did Rimmer take his maintenance course?
12 Where were Lister's sleeping quarters when he first joined *Red Dwarf*?

13 Who had Trixie LaBouche sold her body to for a weekend of lust?

14 Who spontaneously combusted in 1546?

15 Who could go 'straight on the cover of *Vogue*'?

16 How many floors were there down to Floor 16?

17 Whose bunkmate was called Hollerbach?

18 What were the bearings for the Gelf moon?

19 What are the odds of dealing three aces in a row?

20 Which pub was decorated with plastic oak beams?

21 Who was Rimmer's hypnotherapist?

22 On how many occasions did Lister request sick leave due to diarrhoea?

23 Why did Lister owe the Norweb Federation £180 billion?

24 Where were all the captured Gelfs dumped?

25 Whose ident computer was as 'stubborn as a mule'?

26 What's the last thing the simulants would be expecting?

27 What can fissile uranium 233 be synthesized from?

28 Who has a bedside manner like an 'abattoir giblet-gutter'?

29 Which stasis booth should Rimmer have got into?

30 How many strokes did Rimmer's dad have?

31 What was 'Stabim'?

32 Who had a better union than the maintenance personnel?

33 What looked 'like a prize in a gigantic stellar hoop-la game'?

34 Which floor did the meteor hit before Queeg came into power?

35 Whose stuntman did Kryten look like?

36 How long was Better Than Life on the market before being withdrawn?
37 What did the dispenser give Lister instead of a bacon sandwich with French mustard and a black coffee?
38 When did the escape pod 'escape'?
39 Who was left alone with Lister after her father was rushed to hospital with a heart attack?
40 According to Commander Binks, if Lister's actual age is in the mid-twenties, what is his physical age?
41 What was Rimmer's third monstrous ineptitude?
42 According to Holly, what is the lowest form of life in the universe?
43 Who was Miss Lola?
44 Who is the Morale Officer on board *Starbug*?
45 How long did it take Kryten to panel-beat his head back into shape?
46 According to Lister, which team could easily outrun *Starbug*?
47 What year were Phase 4 triple-reinforced-wire telegraph poles introduced?
48 Why do rogue simulants carry large stocks of food supplies?
49 How little sleep did the two Rimmers settle on?
50 Who was the 'greatest American President of all time'?
51 Where did Rimmer hide Kochanski's disc?
52 Who was 'Columbo'?
53 According to Holly, how far were they away from the nearest Berni Inn?
54 Which planet does the Boomerang spoon come from?
55 How many wiring faults did the skutters make?
56 What year would Pluto's solstice be?

57 Where did all the Valkyries go?

58 What was the estimated duration of the dust storm that took place while Lister was suffering from mutated pneumonia?

59 Who was Officer 592?

60 What did young Lister think Rimmer's 'tattoo' stood for?

61 How many questions were in Rimmer's 'initial session'?

62 What did Kryten suggest might have been written on the box that Lister was found in?

63 What is Kryten's full name?

64 How many separate fires did the infra-red report before landing on the Gelf moon?

65 How far was Wax World away from *Red Dwarf*?

66 What does a psi-virus do?

67 According to Rimmer 2, when the going gets tough where do the tough go?

68 Where did Rimmer buy 'for somewhere to go at the weekends'?

69 How many points did Venus score during the voting for Garbage World?

70 Due to the time-dilation effects of the worm hole, how many years did one and a half years equal?

71 Who smashed up the medical unit?

72 Who has got hair like Rimmer's but not on his head?

73 Who said he would use the Ionian nerve grip on Rimmer?

74 How many times was Kryten 'accidentally' shot by the 'Lows'?

75 How did Lister get from Liverpool to the Old Kent Road?

76 What colours did Rimmer paint his Quantum Mechanics revision periods?

77 What did Lister do 'maliciously and persistently' for two years?

78 Who were Juanita's 'shopping pals'?

79 Who was Pierre?

80 Who was Rimmer going to fry like a 'cajun catfish'?

81 Which western did Lister think Rimmer might have watched?

82 Translate into binary: 'Don't stand around jabbering when you're in mortal danger'.

83 How long did it take the private eye to find Lister?

84 According to Holly, who said, 'Hell is being locked for ever in a room with your friends'?

85 When did the Cat call Rimmer 'sir'?

86 How many things had Rimmer achieved on his daily-goal list?

87 What does Rimmer get out of enforcing pernickety regulations?

88 Who owned the toy shop in Bedford Falls?

89 What did Lister want to teleport one more crate of before the ship quake?

90 What was odd about the ship's parrot?

91 Which eye did Lister's future self have missing?

92 Name all three 'Fat Bastards'.

93 Who was the photographer with the box Brownie?

94 Who was the 'Duke of Deliciousness'?

95 According to Rimmer, what were the only two things that his father had ever given him?

96 On which days had Kryten updated the inventory for two million years?

97 Who was 'ippy-dippyed' to death?

98 According to Holly, what were biologically a new life form?

99 What did Rimmer threaten to garotte Lister with?

100 Who was an epileptic?

101 In which school year was Ace kept back at school?

102 What does Kryten prefer to having sex?

103 For how many years running was the 4000 Series voted Android of the Year?

104 How many seats were there in the Copacabana Hawaiian Cocktail Bar?

105 Why did Lister's grandmother 'nut' his headmaster?

106 Whose minds were 'mind-patched' with Rimmer, and what were their IQs?

107 Why was Rimmer beaten at school?

108 Who asked for $17.50 in Frank Capra's *It's a Wonderful Life*?

STAIRCASE 5

When the words listed below are placed horizontally and in the correct order within the grid, they will spell out diagonally (in the boxes marked in bold) another word from *Red Dwarf*.

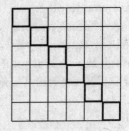

FISHER
HITLER
KRYTEN
LENNON
MILLER
RACHEL

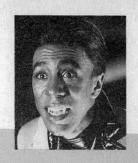

QUESTIONNAIRE

1) Full name. **DANIEL JOHN-JULES**

2) Vital statistics. **Youngish, Freeish, + Singlish**

3) Height. **5'10**

4) Colour of eyes. **Brown**

5) Date of birth. **16 9 60**

6) Place of birth. **LONDON**

7) First job. **STicking LAB**

8) First public appearance. **"NO PLACE FOR US" Commonwealth institute**

9) First big break. **Dancer in THE SECOND GENERATION**

10) Ambition. **TO Be BETTER THAN THE LAST TIME**

11) Hobbies. **MUSIC, CLUBS, Writing, Directing.**

12) If you could play any part, which part would you choose? **ANY PART IN "12 ANGRY MEN" / ANY Part IN "DO THE RIGHT H THING"**

13) Favourite food/drink. **CHICKEN Rice + Peas / 1/2 A GUNESS**

14) Favourite episode of Red Dwarf. **GUNMEN**

15) Least favourite episode of Red Dwarf. **Mmmmm TOUGH ON! Dont know**

16) Favourite T.V. programme(s). **Documentary's**

17) Favourite book. **CAT WATCHING / AUTO Biography**

18) Favourite film. **DO THE RIGHT Thing / MALCOLM X**

19) Person you most admire, past or present. **PAUL ROBESON**

20) Inside leg measurement!!! **34**

CROSSWORD 4
The Cat

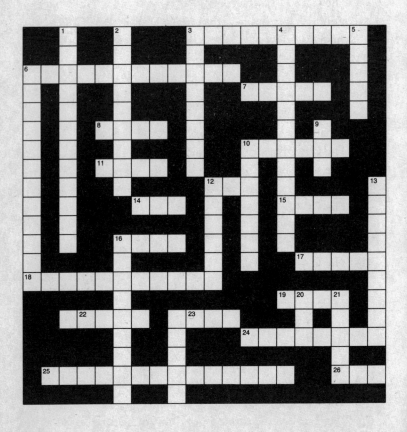

The Questions

Across

3 The Cat's yo-yo (5,5)

6 The Holy Mother of the Cats (12)

7 Duane has a 'dandruff' one of these (5)

8 The Cat's favourite food (4)

10 You'll have trouble getting the Cat away from one of these (6)

11 The Cat is definitely this! (4)

12 The Cat attacked a 'fox' one of these (3)

14 The number of suits the Cat may take into the stasis (3)

15 What is missing from Duane (4)

16 The Cat always carries one of these (4)

17 The school the Cat attended (5)

18 This would be the Cat's middle name (11)

19 The Cat takes plenty of these (4)

22 The Cat has got plenty of this (5)

23 The Cat is averse to this 'W' word (4)

24 The Cat's favourite cereal (8)

25 Too slow for this Cat! (7,7)

26 The Cat's one aim in life is to indulge in this (3)

Down

1 The Cat's geeky ego (5,7)

2 Handy for getting rid of those creases (5,4)

3 The Cat's third favourite activity (8)

4 This marked the turning point in Cat history (7,5)

5 The Cat does this continuously (5)

6 The term for the whole Cat species (5,7)

9 The Cat's 'parallel' opposite (3)
10 One of the Cat's fantasy girlfriends (7)
12 The Promised Land (6)
13 The Cat's scantily clad warriors (9)
16 The Cat even wears these with a spacesuit (9)
20 The Cat has a beautiful one! (3)
21 The Cat has hundreds of these (5)
23 The Christian name of the most desirable woman to have ever lived (5)

OBSERVATION DOME

1 What brand was Lister's chilli powder?
2 What colour is Mimosian telekinetic wine?
3 Which magazine did Sabrina Mulholland-jjones read?
4 What is printed on Rimmer's pyjama pockets?
5 Which letter is being painted in the opening credits?
6 Where did Lister's blanket come from?
7 Which episode did Rob Grant appear in?
8 Which episode carries a warning beforehand?
9 What was the number of the Honeymoon Suite at the Ganymede Holiday Inn?
10 Who was Head of Sales at Divadroid International?
11 What colour was the Cat Priest's hat?
12 Which colour 'ball' did Lister pot into the 'white hole'?
13 How many times did Kryten hit Rimmer with a metal pole?
14 When did Rimmer drink advocaat?
15 Which national flag appears on McIntyre's canister?
16 Which arm did Ace break?
17 How many barrels were stacked up outside the Last Chance Saloon?
18 How many 'selim' are there to 'Nodnol'?
19 What colour was Frankenstein's milk bowl?
20 Who played in the Roof Attack position other than Jim Bexley Speed?
21 Who reads the *Good Schools Guide*?

22 What colour were Kryten's earmuffs?
23 Which magazine was Rimmer reading in the jacuzzi?
24 What material was Petersen's visor made of?
25 Who wore orange armbands?
26 How many buttons were there on Rimmer's dress?
27 In which episodes has Kryten come face to face with himself?
28 In which episode was the last skutter seen?
29 Where was there a model of *Red Dwarf* on board the ship?
30 What is Esperanto for 'level'?
31 What colour was the hankie the Cat offered to leave behind before going into stasis?
32 What did Kryten get as a birthday present?
33 What did Lister turn into after being a chicken?
34 Which condition follows 'marigold'?
35 What colour was Duane Dibbley's toothbrush?
36 What make was Rimmer's cycling helmet?
37 Which level does the Cat first appear on?
38 What was Kochanski's middle initial?
39 What is Esperanto for 'cinema'?
40 How old was Jane Air?
41 Which channel is 'Groovy'?
42 What did Rimmer swap the Ajax for?
43 Which eye of the simulant in the Justice Zone was missing?
44 What is the number of the Quarantine Room?
45 What physical forms appear on the Hologram System Set-up screen?
46 When was the Last Chance Saloon established?
47 What numbers are on the outside of *Starbug*?

48 Who produced and directed *Androids*?

49 What was the registration of Rimmer's E-type Jaguar?

50 What brand of beer do they sell in the George and Dragon?

51 How many books did Lister burn?

52 Where did *The Rocky Horror Show* feature in *Red Dwarf*?

53 What number Total Immersion Video Game were the crew playing?

54 Where were Miss Lola's moles?

55 In which waste disposal unit did Rimmer flush away the gun?

56 What was the make and registration number of Lister's motorcycle?

57 Who features on a poster inside Lister's locker door?

58 Which legs of whom are in plaster?

59 When did Rimmer wear red rubber gloves?

60 How many dog collars did Rimmer wear?

61 What colour was the vase Kryten used in an attempt to knock Rimmer out?

62 When Rimmer started the ship quake, what was the number of the escape pod that he launched?

63 What was Section 14?

64 What colour was the gravel in Lister's fish-tank?

65 Which side is the steering column on *Starbug*?

66 What were the numbers of the skutters who didn't want to be left alone with Rimmer?

67 What make of lager did Lister drink with Lise Yates?

68 Where do Rimmer's 'Armées du Nord' reappear?

69 What per cent was Maximum Enhance?

70 What did the Last Chance Saloon specialize in?

71 What date did the stasis leak happen, and at what time?
72 What is No. 46?
73 What flags did Lister have on his space bike?
74 What did Kryten take asteroid spotting, other than Rimmer and *Starbug*?
75 What western game did they play on the AR machine?
76 What animals did the crew appear to be while in the unreality pocket?
77 Name Rimmer's autobiography.
78 Where was the blue soap?
79 What was odd about the Cat's bouquet of flowers?
80 Which newspaper was the monkey reading on the toilet?
81 Who was Android 241A?
82 What make was the dog food that Lister ate?
83 List all the first Polymorph's disguises.
84 What make of lager killed the Curry Monster?
85 Which ear did Lister stick his cigarette in when playing pool?
86 On which side is 'Low' Lister's eye patch?
87 How would you 'shake hands' with a Gelf?
88 What number waste disposal unit is in the mid-section of *Starbug*?
89 What colour were Rimmer's cycling gloves?
90 'Name' the android in the bus queue.
91 What type of champagne did the Cat steal?
92 What was the colour of the lead that re-boosted Rimmer's battery pack?
93 What make was the indigestion mixture?
94 What colour was Duane's sandwich box?

The Questions

95 What is *Red Dwarf*'s postal address?
96 List, in chronological order, the Emohawk's disguises once aboard *Starbug*.
97 What is No. 129?
98 Which of 'Low' Rimmer's nostrils was pierced?
99 Who caught the bouquet at Lister's wedding?

JIG WORD 3

Take the words from the columns opposite and fit them into the grid wherever space (and sense!) allows, so that they form a crossword.

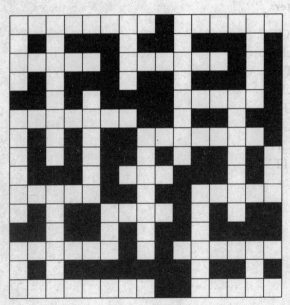

3 Letters

CAT
EWE
HOP
IDA
WAR

4 Letters

DIVA
GIMP
WHIP

5 Letters

EARTH
MAPLE
ORGAN
TEETH
TROUT
YATES

6 Letters

ECHOES
GORDON
GUITAR
HITLER
KIPPER
SATURN
TETCHY
VANITY

7 Letters

CADMIUM
CINZANO
GRENADE
TENSION

8 Letters

GANYMEDE
KRISTINE
NAPOLEON
PARALLEL

MINIMUM LEISURE FACILITIES

1 What was Rimmer's favourite music for love-making?
2 Who sang 'Press Your Lumps Against Mine'?
3 Who starred in the definitive version of *Casablanca*?
4 What is Lister's favourite film?
5 Who played 'Tuneful Tunes for Elderly Ladies'?
6 What was the in-lift movie 'for a small extra charge'?
7 Who sang 'Hey Baby, Don't Be Ovulatin' Tonight'?
8 What is Rimmer's favourite movie?
9 Which song did George McIntyre request for his funeral?
10 Which music is 'off-line' for Kryten?
11 Which films had Lister shown Kryten in order to break his programming?
12 What song did Holly sing before being erased?
13 Which of Kryten's nipples picks up Jazz FM?
14 What music had been linked with disorders of the nervous system and bowel?
15 What was the 'new sensation sweeping the solar system'?
16 What was the first song Lister learnt to play on his guitar?
17 Who played lead guitar in the Cat's band?
18 What night is Amateur Hammond Organ Recital Night?
19 Who had a hit with 'Tango Treats'?

20 What was Holly's first decative composition?
21 Who had a hit with 'Abba Dabba Dabba'?
22 Which company owns the Total Immersion Video
    Games?
23 What video disc was in the video recorder when Lister
    and Rimmer found the Cat city?
24 Whose movies wouldn't you find in Lister's collection?
25 Who had the yellow counters when Rimmer played
    risk while in Better Than Life?
26 Which number *Friday the Thirteenth* is referred to?
27 What was the prize in the prize bingo aboard the
    Nova 5?
28 What dance track was played at Lister's funeral?
29 What sport does Lister like, other than female topless
    boxing?
30 How did Holly's new decative scale run?
31 When did the crew play 'pin the pointy stick on the
    weathergirl'?
32 How many episodes of *Androids* are there?
33 What song did Talkie Toaster sing?
34 Name Perry N'Kwomo's best-selling album?
35 Who did Rimmer stop adoring when he got into
    Rasta Billy Skank?
36 Who played postal chess with Holly?
37 When did Kryten stage his concert parties?
38 Who moved pawn to king four?
39 How many copies of 'Om' did Lister buy?
40 Who wrote 'The Indling Song'?

WORD SEARCH 4
The Rimmers

The words listed opposite are 'hidden' in the grid. They may be found written vertically, horizontally or diagonally, and even backwards.

```
U S P O N T L O U I P S J A C E
Q N I N B A E N T F A N L T O O
F R C A R S H U G G A L I C E K
H O W L A D E S S O N T E A B L
J U E M E O T E H N A B H O H E
A N L O L F R F R O B L S E A N
E J U I A D R A W O H A L A R S
L E N A L R O A S S P E A J H O
M U S T J O E I N I N R E U N E
F R A N K L I C E K D L O E T I
A K X O S P E B L O A T J R A G
C I N E J U M D L O N R A M S G
I T J S O H T A R N O I N S O A
O G L U X H O U A D A F I E B M
L D I T A C U M N O R C N A P E
A R N R J N R A S E P A E N L I
J O A N M O I T H I C E S P A T
D S R A C E P T E I G G J O H N
S O O D F R O N A K X O P D A U
M F R A E M R O L T U A S I V A
```

98

ACE
ALICE
ARLENE
ARNOLD
AUNTIE MAGGIE
FATHER
FRANK
HELEN
HOWARD
JANINE
JOHN
JUANITA
MOTHER
SARAH
UNCLE FRANK

WHO SAID THIS, AND WHERE?
Byte 3

State the characters in *Red Dwarf* who said the following, and in which episodes.

1 'Right, smeg brain, prepare to die.'
2 'We're a real Mickey Mouse operation, aren't we?'
3 'Tomorrow I'm going to see if I can't have sex with something.'
4 'Did you use a set square? I think not.'
5 'A simple yes would have sufficed.'
6 'Reach for the sky, boys. Let me see those understains.'
7 'We're here to entertain ya.'
8 'What's wrong with everyone? Three million years without a woman and you all act as though you're all fourteen years old.'
9 'So you want me to prove it, do you?'
10 'Extrapa-what-alated?'
11 'See you in Silicon Hell.'
12 'You'll never pass, Mr Lister, sir.'
13 'The further thought occurs, that we haven't actually budged a smegging inch.'
14 'It's the state of the floor I'm worried about.'
15 'It's party time for all the little worms.'
16 'Oh smeg! What the smeggin' smeg's he smeggin' done?'
17 'You can't frighten me; I'm a coward.'

18 'I'm almost annoyed.'

19 'Even with an IQ of six thousand, it's still brown trousers time.'

20 'Men. They're all bastards.'

21 'I can't say I'm totally shocked. You'll bonk anything, won't you, Lister?'

22 'That's gone right up my flag-pole, that has, Kryten. I'm saluting that one.'

23 'Are you seriously telling me he's a transvestite, with those hips?'

24 'What have you got? Dinosaur breath, molecule mind, smeg for brains.'

25 'That's it, we're deader than tank tops.'

26 'It really is going to be one of those days, isn't it?'

27 'I'll write you into my will if you let it be me.'

28 'If you're going to eat tuna, expect bones.'

29 'Twinkle, twinkle, little eye. Now it's time for you to die.'

30 'Well, let's see what's in there.'

31 'How can the same smeg happen to the same guy twice?'

32 'He won't find that one; not until he changes his boots.'

33 'Stiff upper modem, old girl.'

34 'I'm fine, thank you, Susan.'

35 'I'm hearing you on FM.'

36 'And what the smeg would *you* know, bog bot from hell?'

37 'Some of us have more important things to do than wiggle our posteriors.'

38 'There's one thing that still baffles me.'

39 'Boy, I'm really getting the hang of this lie mode. That was totally convincing, wasn't it?'
40 'Imagine making love to a woman.'
41 'Take the fifth.'
42 'Don't Nixon me, man.'
43 'The wife will be all white shoes, no tights and blotchy legs.'
44 'Well, I'm sure I have a window in my schedule somewhere.'
45 'Yeah! The Axeman is back.'
46 'I really think.'

1. What were the crew's characters on 'The Streets of Laredo' and what were their special skills? (Photo: Nobby Clark)

2. Who is the Duke of Dork? (Photo: Oliver Upton)

3. Who has got 'early-morning breath that can cut through bank vaults'? (Photo: Mike Vaughan)

4. Who said, 'Excuse me, could I just distract you for a brief second?' (Photo: Mike Vaughan)

5. What was Rimmer's probability of failing the Enlightenment's entry exam? (Photo: Mike Vaughan)

6. Which division of the police force did Jake Bullet work for? (Photo: Mike Vaughan)

7. Whose hat was Rimmer sick into?
(Photo: Oliver Upton)

8. What type of vacation did Rimmer take on board Red Dwarf?
(Photo: Mike Vaughan)

9. What did Talkie Toaster once have an 'accident' with?
(Photo: Mike Vaughan)

10. Which magazine did Rimmer think Ace and Lister
had appeared in? (Photo: Mike Vaughan)

11. What contribution has the Cat made to justify his existence?
(Photo: Mike Vaughan)

12. How long did it take to repair the Hop Drive?
(Photo: Warwick Bedford)

13. Which star sign appears on Rimmer's cycling shirt?
(Photo: Warwick Bedford)

14. How long did Lister actually go out with Kochanski?
(Photo: Oliver Upton)

15. What had a fifteen-zillion gigabyte capacity?
(Photo: Warwick Bedford)

16. What did Rimmer write on his right calf?
(Photo: Warwick Bedford)

OH SMEG INDEED, MATEY!
Megabyte 2

Anybody caught using learning drugs will be put on report!

1 What was Rimmer's Space Scout chant?
2 How many driers were out of commission in the launderettes on East alpha 555?
3 What does Rimmer do to cups when he is tense?
4 What dance do the 'High' Cat and Rimmer perform together?
5 What does 'SWAT' stand for?
6 What was the Cat's 'all-time-best lucky find he ever found in the whole of today'?
7 Who was the Chinese Emperor of the Ming Dynasty in 1620?
8 What did the alien invasion off the starboard bow turn out to be?
9 Where can you take a degree in Advanced Mental Engineering?
10 Who officially opened Garbage World?
11 According to Lister, who constituted the lowest rank on the ship?
12 Without Rimmer's drain on the power, how long would the Cat and Lister last when Holly shuts herself off?
13 Which floor would you go to aboard the *Enlightenment* for Sex and Recreation?

14 Where did Lister claim he was seduced before joining *Red Dwarf*?

15 How does Lister spell 'Thursday'?

16 Don't call Kryten this!

17 On which page did Lister draw beards and moustaches on the sperms?

18 What did Rimmer nearly die of?

19 Where did Saunders come from?

20 Where was the 3000 Series mechanoid made?

21 How many times had Rimmer failed the Engineering exam?

22 What does 'SSM' stand for?

23 What had 'more pages than a James Clavell novel'?

24 What destination on Mimas did Rimmer give when he got into Lister's hopper?

25 Where was Kochanski's mole?

26 What was Carole Brown's clearance code?

27 How many mechanoids does it take to change a light bulb?

28 Who was MTV's second sexiest man of all time?

29 What date was Rimmer's final Astronavigation exam?

30 What did Lister use to pick his ears with?

31 How many years' evolution were there in three solar years when the SSS *Esperanto* tried out a new enhancement technique?

32 What is described as being the size of the north face of the Eiger?

33 Who did Lister's well-chewed, hard ball of gum originally belong to?

34 How far below sea level did Rimmer say the majority of Fiji was?

35 Who did the London Jets play in the European divisional play-offs?

36 According to Lister, what is Rimmer tighter than?

37 What is the penalty for looting Space Corps derelicts?

38 Which cell was Rimmer's essence kept in?

39 What did Rimmer regard as 'not a bad little time for the mile'?

40 By which date had Holly usually forgotten to update his diary?

41 When did Rimmer say he would be up for parole?

42 What does Lister use for picking out his longer nostril hairs?

43 Which machine was dispensing blackcurrant juice instead of chicken soup?

44 What was Todhunter's Christian name?

45 What did 'Senso-lock Feedback Technique' make possible?

46 How many houses did Lister own after he invented the Tension Sheet?

47 According to Rimmer, how many strange individuals had they met on their travels?

48 Who has Trixie LaBouche supposedly done more hooking than?

49 Who called Rimmer 'Rimmer to rhyme with "scum"'?

50 What was in Canister 1121?

51 Which pages of Navigation revision did Queeg give Rimmer to learn?

52 What type are Kryten's eyes?

53 What does a Cat feel in the second minute of a relationship?

54 How many times smarter than the manager of the megamarket did Lister think he was?

55 According to Kochanski, why had Lister been promoted to Admiral?

56 What was it Lister's turn to do on Tuesdays during the power shut-down?

57 According to Holly, how long does your average genus survive?

58 How long had Rimmer been learning Esperanto?

59 What attacked *Starbug* on Christmas Day?

60 What had happened every Friday evening aboard *Red Dwarf* before the accident?

61 How many Sacred Cat Laws were there?

62 How many times did Kochanski dream about Lister?

63 Who was Mrs Harrington?

64 After which switch did the console monitor explode when Lister fixed the Navicomp?

65 What can Planck's Constant never be more than?

66 What caused Kryten's 'double polaroid'?

67 Where did the Gelf rebellion start, and why?

68 What type of car did Rimmer's brother have?

69 Who was likened to the product of a marriage between a woman and a gerbil?

70 Who attempted to poison the source of all the world's Perrier water?

71 Which Psi-scan won 'Best Budget Model' three years running?

72 At what time did Rimmer actually begin his final Astronavigation exam?

73 Which dispenser on Corridor 159 had a clogged chicken-soup nozzle?

74 Who has 'more gut than a Turkish butcher's shop window'?

75 What star sign did Lister claim to be in order to get out of marrying the Gelf?

76 Who owned the pet shop in Bedford Falls?

77 Which of the two Rimmers was to read up on 'metallurgy and thyratron in heat-control systems' when they were revising in the middle of the night?

78 What is stellar fog made of?

79 What did Kryten fantasize he would do to Talkie Toaster?

80 How many hours a day did Rimmer read his course books?

81 On what date did Rimmer suggest Scott bludgeoned Oates to death?

82 Who did Rimmer accuse of being a necrophiliac?

83 What did Rimmer and Albert Einstein agree on?

84 What was the penalty for Cats who were vain?

85 How will Satan be going to work when Lister becomes an officer?

86 What does 'GAS' stand for?

87 At what time during his concert party did Kryten tap-dance on to his makeshift stage?

88 What ingredients does Rimmer possess which result in him being a 'total smeghead'?

89 Where was the exam hall on *Red Dwarf*?

90 What did Lister once call his gym master?

91 How many hours' sleep did the two Rimmers have in twenty-one days?

92 Which club did Hudzen go to in *Androids*?

93 What was the 'ultimate humiliation' for Hammy?

94 How many teeth did the Polymorph have?

95 Name Rimmer's cousins.

96 Which arm was Lister's missing watch on?

97 How long did it take Kryten to reconnect his circuitry after sawing himself in half?

98 What did Lister think was a souvenir from Titan Zoo?

99 What time was supper three for the two Rimmers?

100 Which photographic shot does everyone take?

101 Who was Kochanski's bunk-mate?

102 Who left Benzen?

103 How long were Cat and Lister in a stasis seal while their future selves were on board *Starbug*?

104 How long does a Cat relationship last?

105 Who thought he was a moose?

106 Where on *Red Dwarf* would you find pin-ups of John Wayne?

QUESTIONNAIRE

1) Full name. ROBERT LLEWELLYN

2) Vital statistics. KNACKERED

3) Height. 6 foot

4) Colour of eyes. Blue

5) Date of birth. 10th March 1956

6) Place of birth. NORTHAMPTON

7) First job. BATTERY CHICKEN FARM

8) First public appearance. WATERSIDE THEATRE – 1979

9) First big break. CO-WROTE – CO-PRODUCED – CO-STARRED IN C4 SIT COM – "THE CORNERHOUSE"

10) Ambition. TO BUILD MY OWN HOUSE AND LEARN TO SWIM

11) Hobbies. GARDENING – COOKING – TALKING – SHOWING OFF – BEING CHEAP IN PUBLIC

12) If you could play any part, which part would you choose?

....

....

13) Favourite food/ drink. FRESH TUNA SALAD – FRESH SQUEEZED PEAR AND GRAPE JUICE

14) Favourite episode of Red Dwarf. } HONESTLY CAN'T REMEMBER – HAVE BRIAN LIKE SIEVE.

15) Least favourite episode of Red Dwarf.

16) Favourite T.V. programme(s). HEAVY DOCUMENTARYS ABOUT WAR CRIME, DRUGS, DEFORESTATION

17) Favourite book. DAMAGE – JOSEPHINE HART

18) Favourite film. APOCALYPSE NOW

19) Person you most admire, past or present. GHANDI

20) Inside leg measurement!!! BLOODY LONG – 37 inches I think

CROSSWORD 5
Kryten

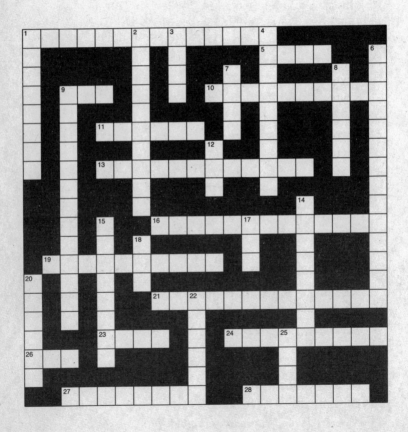

Across

1 This was caused by a turbo-vac (6,8)
5 Kryten just loves to do this (4)
9 What Kryten calls Dave Lister (3)
10 This type of music's 'off-line' for Kryten (10)
11 Don't call Kryten this! (6)
13 Jake Bullet's division (12)
16 Where to plug in an egg whisk (7,6)
19 Kryten's alter ego (4,6)
21 Kryten's war-time code name (4,9)
23 See 20 down
24 Kryten's replacement (6,3)
26 Kryten's just not programmed to do this (3)
27 Kryten's favourite TV show (8)
28 Kryten's *Casablanca* love (7)

Down

1 Spare head three suffers from this (5,3)
2 The venue for Kryten's 'date' (7,3)
3 What the iron will lie down with (4)
4 Kryten's rental company (9)
6 He talks with a northern accent (5,4,5)
7 Kryten loves the squeezy type of these (4)
8 This is broadcast from Kryten's left nipple (4–2)
9 Where all the calculators go (7,6)
12 The only dance Kryten knows (3)
14 Where Kryten originally served (4,4)
15 Kryten derives orgasmic pleasure from this activity! (8)
17 Kryten had a medium-sized one in his back (3)

18 Kryten never had one of these (3)
20 and 23 across. Spin these and you'll send Kryten to Alaska (6,4)
22 Kryten does this to everything in sight (6)
25 Kryten's eyes are fitted with this function (4)

NON-REGISTERED
CREW MEMBERS
Byte 4

Match the guest stars with the characters they played.

1	Roger Blake	a	New Kochanski ('Back
2	David Gillespie		to Reality')
3	Mark Williams	b	Pete Tranter's sister
4	Louisa Ruthren	c	Pub manager
5	Gordon Kennedy	d	George McIntyre
6	Kenneth Hadley	e	Thomas Allman
7	Robert McCulley	f	Selby
8	Hetty Baynes	g	Noël Coward
9	James Cormack	h	Adolf Hitler
10	James Smillie	i	Ski woman
11	Stephen McKintosh	j	Gelf Chief
12	Anastasia Hille	k	Petersen
13	Michael Burrell	l	Loretta
14	John Docherty	m	Ace's cockpit computer
15	Richard Ridings	n	Fred 'Thicky' Holden
16	Marie McCarthy	o	Recuperation nurse
17	Arthur Smith	p	The Inquisitor
18	Samantha Robson	q	Justice computer voice
19	Jennifer Calvert	r	Pope Gregory
20	Ainsley Harriott	s	DNA computer voice
		t	Hudzen 10

WORD SEARCH 5
Famous people

The words listed opposite are 'hidden' in the grid. They may be found written vertically, horizontally or diagonally, and even backwards.

```
H A M M Y H A M S T E R S T I G
C I S O A D F R O O N I E S P K
O I T S S H A P I R O T T E R E
T S A L C B G O N I T U P S A R
A S N O E L D E E T S P U R J U
C S L A T R R L Y A T M S O O L
K G A N D H I N N O N E A S T C
R O U N S P E C A L I G U L A C
R A R O O N O N N E L O K L U M
I Q E S P E U H S E F A A F J G
C O L U M B O K N P A O F Q E U
H A P D I J O M I G M I E M S O
A S T T O Q I A J K L O A A P D
R A D N N L H R O C I S U T T P
D S S O L A A I N T W A Y N E S
F K J E A G E L V I S G E H U Q
E O R N O M K Y O O A T E S O A
E R S S E R S N A P O L E O N D
T S H O J T T O E I E L C P A O
D R A W O C I L T N A S E M A J
```

The Questions

CALIGULA
CLIFF RICHARD
COLUMBO
DOUG McCLURE
ELVIS
GANDHI
GLEN MILLER
HAMMY HAMSTER
HELEN SHAPIRO
HITLER
JAMES LAST
JOHN WAYNE
LENNON
MARILYN MONROE
NAPOLEON
NOEL COWARD
RASPUTIN
STAN LAUREL
WILMA FLINTSTONE

WHO SAID THIS, AND WHERE?
Byte 4

State the characters in *Red Dwarf* who said the following, and in which episodes.

1 'I'm turning into Hugh Hefner.'
2 'This is a very, very bad dream, right?'
3 'Screw down my diodes and call me Frank.'
4 'You've never got time for people. You're too busy trying to be successful. It's all midnight revision and up, up, up the ziggurat, lickety-split.'
5 'Do me a lemon.'
6 'I didn't even know they had a duty-free shop.'
7 'Unpack Rachel and get out the puncture-repair kit.'
8 'I am what I am!'
9 'How can you make a space suit look like evening wear?'
10 'Might I suggest that, from this moment on, the rest of this discourse is conducted by those with brains larger than a grape?'
11 'Is that you, Mother?'
12 'He's your father? No wonder you so ugly.'
13 'Well, you see, the shuttle was late.'
14 'Be ya later.'
15 'I'm not a combination of the speaking clock, Moss Bros and Teasy Weasy.'
16 'They're maladjusted.'

17 'Nobody's rearranging my molecules.'

18 'I'm sorry, sirs; I had no choice. I'm programmed to obey, no matter how psychotic and deranged the human order.'

19 'Kryten, sit down. I'm not doing my own smegging ironing.'

20 'Well, it just makes me bitter.'

21 'Go for your guns, you scum-sucking molluscs.'

22 'This must seem pretty spooky for everyone.'

23 'I don't want to spread any panic or alarm.'

24 'Come on, Listy. You've dated worse.'

25 'There's a wise old Cat saying which I think applies in this situation. It goes: "What are you talking about, dog breath?"'

26 'Lister, you'll die for this.'

27 'After you with the balls, sir.'

28 'Face it, we're deader than corduroy.'

29 'Have you any idea what kind of day I've had?'

30 'So, you dog, you're back.'

31 'I'm looking nice. My hair's nice, my face is nice, my suit is nice. I'm looking really nice.'

32 'You think I need your help? You think I can't extract my own head from the waste disposal unit?'

33 'Look at you. You're turning into a sad, middle-aged woman. Next thing you know, you'll be varnishing your nails and buying girdles.'

34 'I've forgotten what I was going to say.'

35 'Well, I tried to wake you up in the spring but you absolutely insisted on another three months.'

36 'Not the way spanners behave in my book.'

37 'Innards and lavender? I think I can carry that off.'

38 'We can't possibly do that. Who'd clear up the mess?'
39 'Have infection, will travel.'
40 'Smooth, with a capital "smoo".'
41 'And what's his mission? To rid the universe of chicken vindaloo?'
42 'Boy, this is worse than triple-strength cat nip.'
43 'There's no need for you to sling your love spuds on the barbecue.'
44 'It's not that easy, Kryten. You can't see what she's doing with her pointy stick.'
45 'Isn't that a urine stain on your trousers?'
46 'Hook, line, sinker, rod and copy of *Angling Times*, sir.'

STAIRCASE 6

When the words listed below are placed horizontally and in the correct order within the grid, they will spell out diagonally (in the boxes marked in bold) another word from *Red Dwarf*.

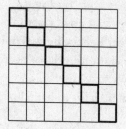

ALBERT
AWOOGA
DUNCAN
GROOVY
INGRID
PADDLE

GIRLS FROM THE *DWARF*

1 What was Saunders's wife called?
2 Who was the recipient of Rimmer's secret love letters?
3 Who did Lister lose his virginity to?
4 Who did Rimmer get off with in his dad's greenhouse?
5 What is the binary code for love?
6 Who had an 'artificial nose, tastefully done, no rivets'?
7 Who did Rimmer believe he was in love with after Lister gave him eight months of his memory?
8 Who was Holly's first love?
9 Who did Rimmer claim to have lost his virginity to at cadet college?
10 What are the two types of women that Lister always falls for?
11 Who was Rimmer's second wife?
12 Who did Yvonne McGruder think she was making love to?
13 Who was the daughter of the Duke of Lincoln?
14 Who was Ingrid?
15 Who dated Jim Bexley Speed?
16 Who gave Rimmer his first French kiss?
17 Who did Rimmer think Camille looked like?
18 Who offered to be covered in maple syrup?
19 Who did Rimmer dance the Black Bottom with?
20 How many children did Rimmer and McGruder have?

21 Who did Lister lust after throughout his puberty?
22 Who was a 'psychopathic, schizophrenic serial-killing *femme fatale*'?
23 Whose wife was an 'absolute cutie'?
24 According to the Cat, who is the most desirable woman to have ever lived?
25 Who sacrificed her life for Rimmer?
26 Who did Juanita get engaged to after divorcing Rimmer?
27 Exactly how long did Rimmer make love to Yvonne McGruder, and what was the date?
28 Who was married to Hector?
29 Which one of his cousins was Rimmer sure fancied him?

WORD SEARCH 6
Animals from the Dwarf

The words listed opposite are 'hidden' in the grid. They may be found written vertically, horizontally or diagonally, and even backwards.

```
A A R D V A R K S T O A E N T C
L L A G A L K O M A D V O D R O
L U W D O L A M B R O M O U S G
G O I M T I E S S D R T N I O N
C A T C R G B I T O M A D A S I
O L A D D A O C T U O R T Q K M
K J R E N T B O O C U T U G O A
T R A O T O S B T P S A M B T L
A S N W A R P D I V E O F L D F
D U T O R G E R A T B N M O A D
R N U U T S F O C M G O G D I S
E K L E R R I U Q S E N U U I M
J I A N O T A S E N G U N E I O
N C C G U R T A O L O A G L L N
A U S X A C Q E U R L E L F R K
I R E D I F K C O D D A H B O E
N O E I L A O G L D F J E D R Y
A T A R N I W T A P I M O A B O
R E T S M A H A D D S Q U I D O
I K Q U I O S G O L H O A S T D
```

122

AARDVARK
ALLIGATOR
CAT
COW
DOG
DORMOUSE
DOVE
FLAMINGO
FROGS
GOAT
GOLDFISH
HADDOCK
HAMSTER
IRANIAN JERD
LAMB
MONKEY
PENGUIN
PRAWN
RABBIT
SQUID
SQUIRREL
SNAKE
TARANTULA
TROUT

OH SMEG INDEED, MATEY!
Megabyte 3

Goat vindaloo on your revision timetable is *not* an excuse for failing your exams!

1. What was the Love Celibacy Society's philosophy?
2. Where was the New Zodiac Festival held?
3. Who was Sydney?
4. Who went on Rimmer's stag night?
5. When did Lister call Rimmer a 'nice guy'?
6. What did the 'iron' lie down with?
7. How much did it cost to write 'Coke Adds Life'?
8. In Rimmer's divorce case, what was Exhibit B?
9. Why did Lister once wish he was a squirrel?
10. What is the entire panel described as deader than when being snared by Legion?
11. What did Lister give Rimmer instead of a 14B?
12. Who 'goes down under'?
13. What did the escort agency turn into?
14. Why wasn't Rimmer allowed to go to the Russian circus?
15. What were 'as rare as Venus's arms'?
16. What is a gestalt entity?
17. What was the worst thing Kochanski could have said if Lister had asked her out?
18. What is like a 'gigantic version of the Barbican Centre'?

19 What did Lister never buy because he was saving up?

20 How high was Kryten's embarrassment factor when he got drunk?

21 What do mechanoids normally do in private?

22 What did Rimmer find in his coffee mug when Lister was repairing Kryten?

23 Which deck is the Penthouse Suite on?

24 What are 'waterproof and chewable'?

25 Where did Lister get the learning drugs from?

26 What did Kryten do in the middle of Marlon Brando's rebel speech?

27 Who was Nancy O'Keefe?

28 How old was Lister when he was abandoned as a baby?

29 What was the surprise in the middle of the tin cans and banana peel?

30 What was at the epicentre of the reality minefield?

31 What cost $£4.30?

32 Who was 'Mr Mongolia'?

33 What happened in twelfth-century Burgundy?

34 What position did Rimmer hold in the Hammond Organ Owners' Society?

35 In which century was the seeding ship looted by the rogue simulants constructed?

36 When was Rimmer in 'total comfac of his mandulties'?

37 How many miles was Lister away from Liverpool when he first joined *Red Dwarf*?

38 What group was Rimmer once a member of?

39 Where did Lister always go on a Sunday afternoon?

40 What was Lister's quantum probability in stasis?

41 According to Holly, when would the reverse thrust take effect?

42 What did Valter Holman kill?

43 How many times had Rimmer taken and failed the Astronavigation exam?

44 According to Lister, what languages do the crew not speak?

45 What is Rimmer allergic to?

46 What did the Cat 'read' in Lister's dirty washing?

47 Where did Lister and Kryten find the Cat when they wanted to go mining?

48 According to Rimmer, which side has won every major battle in history?

49 Who was in charge of 'Security and Surveillance'?

50 Who 'worked on the invitations' for Kryten's party?

51 Who had a crew cut?

52 When did Rimmer dance the flamenco?

53 How many delivery boys did Juanita have affairs with?

54 What was in Bay 47?

55 Who did Lister try the 'intelligence test' on?

56 For what time did Rimmer set the sonic-boom extra-loud emergency alarm?

57 When and where had the twenty-eighth-century derelict contracted an influenza virus?

58 What are 'necrobics'?

59 How many dollars did the 'fat guy' in *It's a Wonderful Life* want?

60 Who refused a blindfold?

61 Who was Crew No. 4172?

62 What did Ace say to Duane was a 'small price to pay for saving their chummies'?

63 Which computer went 'doo-lally'?

64 What hasn't Lister done in one leap ice-age?

65 How many terms did Rimmer take to make a tent peg?

66 How old was the ball girl in the Wimbledon game?

67 According to Rimmer, which passage of the Bible is 'Faith, Hop and Charity' from?

68 How many Saatchis were there at the advertising agency that was behind the Coke campaign?

69 When was Rimmer's Auntie Maggie's birthday?

70 What time was it when Rimmer wanted to be erased?

71 What speed did Ace have to travel to reach a parallel universe?

72 Who did Cat advise Lister to ask for help with the 'taranshula'?

73 Why didn't Lister read any books?

74 After the *Nova 5* had crashed, how far away were Kryten's legs from the rest of his body?

75 Where was the vase of jasmine?

76 How did Rimmer cheat in his eye test?

77 Why did Lister spend six weeks in traction?

78 Who had blood type 'A'?

79 Which foot jiggles when Kryten is lying?

80 How many skutters went mining with Lister, Kryten and the Cat?

81 What channel did the pilot's headset get jammed on?

82 Where did the Time Drive first take the crew?

83 Where did Lister get the photo of Kochanski that he had on Garbage World?

84 How much was a week's takings at Bailey's Perfect Shami Kebab Emporium?

85 What is 'tougher than vindalooed mutton'?

86 Who ate his own feet?
87 At what time did the two Rimmers go to bed on the first night?
88 Who was Horace?
89 What did the 'wrong number' phone up for when Rimmer was at the Samaritans?
90 What did Lister have a 'gift for'?
91 What is Lister's security code?
92 Where might you expect to find a 'Turner seascape'?
93 What can't goldfish be trusted to do?
94 What was the third Cat Commandment?
95 What is 'as plain as a Bulgarian pin-up'?
96 What did Cat's nostril hair 'shimmy' faster than?
97 How long was it until the fuel tanks on *Starbug* would have exploded on the Psi-moon?
98 How tall was the snowman on Lister's lawn in Bedford Falls?
99 On which floor were the Botanical Gardens aboard the *Enlightenment*?
100 How many pairs of oven gloves did Kryten wear to take out Lister's kebabs?
101 When does Kryten get 'a little emotional'?
102 Which planetary Immigration Control is worse than New York's?
103 Who was Bing Baxter?
104 How long did Rimmer once wait outside a cinema?
105 Who was xenophobic?
106 Who believes in reincarnation?
107 What were the two pimps having a disagreement about?
108 How many megabytes of data did *Red Dwarf*'s Navicomp have?

QUESTIONNAIRE

1) Full name. ROBERT GRANT

2) Vital statistics. V. VARIABLE

3) Height. JUST UNDER 6' IF YOU SQUINT

4) Colour of eyes. MUD

5) Date of birth. COME ON

6) Place of birth. SALFORD

7) First job. ~~PAPERBOY~~

8) First material broadcast. T' RADIO SKETCH 'THE BIG MELT' (A CHANDLER PARODY)

9) Ambition. TO BE PAID FOR EATING INDIAN FOOD

10) Hobbies. WORK

11) Is there anything that you have edited out from an episode that you wished you had left in?
LOTS. MOST RECENTLY A ~~BREATHING~~ DUANE DIBBLEY SEQUENCE ABOUT HIS YO-YO IN 'EMOHAWK'

12) Favourite food/drink. INDIAN FOOD / POTATOES / CIDER

13) Favourite episode of Red Dwarf. FUTURE ECHOES / FIRST 10 MINS OF 'LEGION'

14) Least favourite episode of Red Dwarf. 'WAITING FOR GOD'

15) Favourite T.V. programme(s). CRACKER / STAR TREK (NEXT GEN) / TWIN PEAKS

16) Favourite book. 'I CLAUDIUS'

17) Favourite film. IT'S A WONDERFUL LIFE

18) Person you most admire, past or present.
WOODY ALLEN / DAVID MAMET

QUESTIONNAIRE

1) Full name. DOUGLAS NAYLOR

2) Vital statistics. BLUBBERY

3) Height. IN FOUR INCH STILETTOS - 6 FT

4) Colour of eyes. RED

5) Date of birth. SOMETHING B.C.

6) Place of birth. BETWEEN MOTHER'S LEGS

7) First job. ICE CREAM SALES OPERATIVE

8) First material broadcast. 'BIG MELT' SKETCH FOR RADIO 4 COMEDY SHOW

9) Ambition. TO FILL IN QUESTIONNAIRES AS FULL TIME JOB

10) Hobbies. DRESSING UP AS JULIE ANDREWS AND SINGING HITS FROM THE SOUND OF MUSIC

11) Is there anything that you have edited out from an episode that you wished you had left in?

DIANE DIABLEY SEQUENCE FROM 'EMOHAWK'

12) Favourite food/drink. CHICKEN MADRAS / MILK SHAKES / ALKA SELTZER

13) Favourite episode of Red Dwarf. THE ONE WE'RE ABOUT TO WRITE

14) Least favourite episode of Red Dwarf. MOST OF SERIES I

15) Favourite T.V. programme(s). 'I CLAUDIUS', 'CHEERS', 'EDGE OF DARKNESS'

16) Favourite book. CHANDLER, TOLSTOY, P.G. WODEHOUSE

17) Favourite film. 'IT'S A WONDERFUL LIFE'

18) Person you most admire, past or present.

ANYONE WHO CAN READ MY WRITING

STAIRCASE 7

When the words listed below are placed horizontally and in the correct order within the grid, they will spell out diagonally (in the boxes marked in bold) another word from *Red Dwarf*.

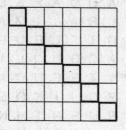

ALIENS
AWOOGA
BEXLEY
DONALD
MONKEY
SATURN

WORD SEARCH 7
Duane Dibbley

The words listed opposite are 'hidden' in the grid. They may be found written vertically, horizontally or diagonally, and even backwards.

```
P O L Y M O R P H O Y A S T B A
D L N D S A D O A P S D O F O N
A K A E C L R A L I M A N F S I
S M G S P O T T L E U P J U B M
B A I P T A C D U D L I Q R I A
R S D A T I T E C D C A U D U L
I A R I D P C U I K O S S N S F
N I A R T S U S N T H N R A E O
Y K C Q P O O Q A S H T E D E O
L O H A I R C U T N B O T A M T
O A T F U N T I I O D M S O S P
N Q U I S D F D O A B A A L T R
J G E E K Y E E N U P T L A O I
O A D Y T P Q X I O P A P S V N
K C D U O I O U Q P T E N O I T
A T O O T H B R U S H S R E N C
R E R K C A P R O T A N O N U H
O A K D S I O R E R E C C O B A
N R O I V O N E I V Q R O S T R
A N N A A O T E P S O M R E H T
```

132

The Questions

ANIMAL FOOTPRINT CHART
ANORAK
BASIN HAIRCUT
BRI NYLON
CAT
CARDIGAN
CLUMSY
CORN PLASTERS
DANDRUFF BRUSH
DESPAIR SQUID
DORK
GEEKY
HALLUCINATION
OVERBITE
PLASTIC SANDALS
POLYMORPH
TEETH
THERMOS
TOOTHBRUSH

**Well, smeghead – how much
did you smegging well know, then?**

or

THE ANSWERS

Please note that sources are provided in brackets following certain sections of the Answers. These refer either to episodes of *Red Dwarf* (e.g. 'Marooned', 'Stasis Leak') or to the *Red Dwarf* novels (i.e. *Red Dwarf: Infinity Welcomes Careful Drivers*, shortened here to *Infinity*; *Better Than Life*, shortened to *BTL*; and *Red Dwarf Omnibus* shortened to *Omnibus*), all published by Penguin Books. In some cases, two references are provided (to an episode and to one of the novels), and sometimes, just to complicate matters, there are two answers to a single question.

SMEG!

1 John, Howard and Frank (*Infinity*, p. 61)
2 Holly ('Queeg')
3 Lister ('Marooned' or *BTL*, p. 114)
4 Hudzen 10 ('The Last Day')
5 Legion ('Legion')
6 Lennon and McCartney ('Future Echoes' or *Infinity*, p. 112)
7 Two ('Quarantine')
8 Floor 16 ('Stasis Leak')
9 Droid rot ('DNA')
10 'You' ('Thanks for the Memory')
11 Hugo, the pool man (*Infinity*, p. 268)
12 Loretta ('Gunmen of the Apocalypse')

13 $£19.99 plus tax ('White Hole' or *BTL*, p. 157)
14 On Fiji ('The End')
15 A garbage pod ('Waiting for God')
16 'The Sensational Reverse Brothers' or 'srehtorB
    esreveR lanoitasneS ehT' ('Backwards')
17 Helen Shapiro ('Future Echoes')
18 Rasta Billy Skank ('Dimension Jump')
19 Because he was a hologram ('Justice')
20 Four ('Gunmen of the Apocalypse')
21 220 Sycamore Avenue, Bedford Falls (*Infinity*, p. 261)
22 Kochanski's ('Balance of Power')
23 Captain Hollister ('Stasis Leak')
24 25 November ('Me²')
25 Cars ('Justice')
26 The 'Lows' ('Demons and Angels')
27 JOZXYQK ('Bodyswap')
28 No. 4179 (*Infinity*, p. 35)
29 Lister as a mate for the Chief's daughter ('Emohawk –
    Polymorph II')
30 Duane Dibbley ('Back to Reality')
31 Fifty ('Meltdown')
32 Kath and Linda (*Infinity*, dedication page)
33 Channel 27 ('Future Echoes')
34 Six hundred years ('Rimmerworld')
35 The Chef's exam ('Balance of Power')
36 Fifteen ('Out of Time')
37 The Drive Room (*Infinity*, p. 81)
38 A two-pound black-ribbed knobbler ('Dimension
    Jump')
39 'The cripple and the idiot' ('Waiting for God' or
    Infinity, p. 125)

40 Confidence ('Confidence and Paranoia')

41 Shaving foam ('Future Echoes')

42 Duane Dibbley ('Emohawk – Polymorph II')

43 All six of his nipples tingle ('Kryten' or *Infinity*, p. 176)

44 Rimmer ('The End')

45 Nellie Armstrong ('Parallel Universe')

46 Grit ('Marooned')

47 Io (*Infinity*, p. 61)

48 Death, War, Famine and Pestilence ('Gunmen of the Apocalypse')

49 He dropped it into his mug ('Bodyswap')

50 Yakka Takka Tulla ('Queeg')

51 His kidney ('Psirens')

52 A banana ('Camille')

53 Rimmer ('Justice')

54 'Bronze Swimming Certificate' and 'Silver Swimming Certificate' ('Me²')

55 Because rubber shares went up that morning ('Dimension Jump')

56 A snow plough (*Infinity*, p. 62)

57 In Prehistoric World ('Meltdown')

58 Jenna Russell, or Clayton Mark as Elvis, or the skutters play it on a Hammond organ

59 Cloister the Stupid ('Waiting for God') or Cloister or Clister (*Infinity*, p. 124)

60 Charm ('Terrorform')

61 Rimmer ('Back to Reality')

62 Jupiter (*Infinity*, p. 61)

63 The King of the Potato People ('Quarantine')

64 WD40 ('Camille')

65 Holly ('Queeg')

66 Jonathan ('The Inquisitor')
67 Ruby Wax ('Timeslides')
68 Flock wallpaper ('DNA')
69 Commander Binks ('Holoship')
70 Rimmer's mum ('The Inquisitor')
71 Lemming Sunday ('The Last Day')
72 Madras sauce ('Bodyswap')
73 Three million(ish) (Series I onwards)
74 Doves ('Gunmen of the Apocalypse')
75 An orange ('Camille')
76 Emily Berkenstein's (*Infinity*, p. 36)
77 To lead a worthwhile life ('The Inquisitor')
78 A roast chicken ('Waiting for God')
79 The fish earring he really hates ('The Last Day')
80 Lager ('DNA')
81 Orange (*Infinity* and *BTL*, biography pages)
82 In an emergency (*Infinity*, p. 50)
83 Hammy Hamster ('Camille')
84 C. P. Grogan ('The End', 'Balance of Power', 'Stasis Leak', 'Psirens')
85 Eight o'clock ('Camille')
86 Kryten ('Bodyswap')
87 Hollister ('The End') or Kirk (*Infinity* p. 56)
88 Because he is programmed not to kill ('The Inquisitor')
89 'Half-brothers, uterinal' ('Back to Reality')
90 A thermos, sandwiches, cornplasters, telephone money, a dandruff brush, an animal-footprint chart and one triple-thick condom ('Emohawk – Polymorph II')
91 Ninety-seven minutes ('Kryten' or *Infinity*, p. 171)
92 Eight (two Sundays) (*Infinity*, p. 16)
93 Dignity ('Gunmen of the Apocalypse')

94 Dobbin ('Timeslides')

95 Eighty-four ('Quarantine')

96 Lister ('The End')

97 Slumped across a table in McDonald's (*Infinity*, p. 13)

98 Phillip ('Gunmen of the Apocalypse')

99 'Superficial' ('Back to Reality')

100 Because he considered him the best person to keep Lister sane ('Balance of Power' or *Infinity*, p. 104)

101 Second Technician (Series I onwards) or First Technician (*Infinity*, p. 46)

102 Two hours ('The Last Day')

103 By clapping your hands ('Gunmen of the Apocalypse')

104 'Genetically Engineered Life Form' ('Camille' or *BTL*, p. 173)

105 Eight ('Justice')

106 Rimmer ('Polymorph')

107 Io House ('Dimension Jump')

108 Trolley Attendant ('Waiting for God' or *Infinity*, p. 149)

109 Six ('Queeg')

110 A three-dimensional sculpture ('Legion')

111 A yo-yo ('Waiting for God')

112 Sleeping ('Thanks for the Memory' or *Infinity*, p. 216)

113 Many centuries ('Legion')

114 Himself ('Timeslides')

115 Cut a brick in half ('The Last Day')

116 An Oxy-Generation Unit ('Emohawk – Polymorph II')

117 Four hundred ('The End') or five hundred (*Infinity*, p. 65)

118 Estonia ('Dimension Jump' or *Infinity*, p. 38)
119 Lister and the Cat ('Backwards')

CROSSWORD 1

Rimmer

STAIRCASE 1

G	I	L	B	E	R	T
S	I	L	I	C	O	N
C	A	M	I	L	L	E
R	O	E	B	U	C	K
P	A	R	R	O	T	S
C	A	P	T	A	I	N
H	A	M	M	O	N	D

WHO SAID THIS, AND WHERE?
Byte 1

1 Rimmer ('Timeslides')
2 The Cat ('White Hole')
3 Rimmer ('Kryten')
4 Kryten ('The Last Day')
5 Lister ('Bodyswap')
6 Rimmer ('DNA')
7 Holly ('White Hole')
8 Lister ('The Inquisitor')
9 Rimmer ('Dimension Jump')
10 Hudzen ('The Last Day')
11 The Cat ('Meltdown')
12 Kryten ('The Inquisitor')
13 Lister ('The End')

14 Gordon ('Better Than Life')
15 Rimmer ('Emohawk – Polymorph II')
16 Rimmer ('Stasis Leak')
17 Holly ('Stasis Leak')
18 Lister ('Me²')
19 Lister ('Legion')
20 Kryten ('Kryten')
21 The Cat ('Terrorform')
22 The Cat ('Back to Reality')
23 Holly ('Dimension Jump')
24 Talkie Toaster ('Waiting for God')
25 Rimmer ('Legion')
26 Rimmer ('Parallel Universe')
27 Lister ('The Last Day')
28 Kryten ('Legion')
29 The Cat ('The End')
30 Rimmer ('Emohawk – Polymorph II')
31 Kryten ('Polymorph')
32 Mr Flibble ('Quarantine')
33 The Cat ('Justice')
34 Rimmer ('Out of Time')
35 Lister ('Backwards')
36 Kryten ('Justice')
37 Holly ('Backwards')
38 The Cat ('Polymorph')
39 Loretta ('Gunmen of the Apocalypse')
40 Rimmer ('Waiting for God')
41 Kryten ('DNA')
42 The Cat ('Better Than Life')
43 Kochanski ('Psirens')
44 Rimmer ('Future Echoes')

45 The Cat ('Gunmen of the Apocalypse')
46 Lister ('Rimmerworld')

NON-REGISTERED
CREW MEMBERS
Byte 1

1 – i		11 – e
2 – j		12 – p
3 – h		13 – q
4 – k		14 – t
5 – g		15 – s
6 – a		16 – r
7 – d		17 – n
8 – c		18 – o
9 – f		19 – m
10 – b		20 – l

WORD SEARCH 1

Happy hour

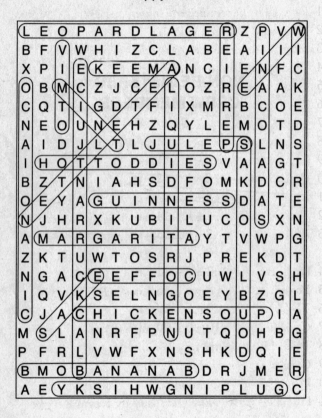

```
L E O P A R D L A G E R Z P V W
B F V W H I Z C L A B E A I I I
X P I E K E E M A N C I E N F C
O B M C Z J C E L O Z R E A A K
C Q T I G D T F I X M R B C O E
N E O U N E H Z Q Y L E M O T D
A I D J L T L J U L E P S L N S
I H O T T O D D I E S V A G T T
B Z T N I A H S D F O M K D C R
O E Y A G U I N N E S S D A T E
N J H R X K U B I L U C O S X N
A M A R G A R I T A Y T V W P G
Z K T U W T O S R J P R E K D T
N G A C E E F F O C U W L V S H
I Q V K S E L N G O E Y B Z G L
C J A C H I C K E N S O U P I A
M S L A N R F P N U T Q O H B G
P F R L V W F X N S H K D Q I E
B M O B A N A N A B D R J M E R
A E Y K S I H W G N I P L U G C
```

'I'VE NEVER READ . . . A BOOK'

1 Page 78 in *Florentine Art* (*Infinity*, p. 232)
2 *Survivalist* (*Infinity*, p. 203)
3 One hundred and twenty (*Infinity*, p. 38)
4 Vladimir Nabokov (*Infinity*, p. 101)
5 Netta Muskett's (*Infinity*, p. 122)
6 *The Genetic Cloning Manual* ('Rimmerworld')
7 Fifteen (*Infinity*, p. 104)
8 'To my darling Candy' ('Better Than Life')
9 Jeremy Greer ('Parallel Universe')
10 Page 61 ('Marooned')
11 *How to Pick Up Girls by Hypnosis* ('Parallel Universe')
12 *The Junior (Colour) Encyclopedia of Space* ('Queeg')
13 *How to Overcome Your Fear of Speaking in Public*
   (*Infinity*, p. 48)
14 Dr P. Brewis (*Infinity*, p. 67)
15 *Young, Bad and Dangerous to Know*, (*BTL*, p. 55)
16 *The A–Z of Red Dwarf* ('Me²')
17 *Camera Monthly* ('Parallel Universe')
18 Three hundred and fifty (*Infinity*, p. 111)
19 *Combat and Survival* (*BTL*, p. 54)
20 *What Carcass?* ('Quarantine')
21 *Football – It's a Funny Old Game* by Kevin Keegan
   ('Confidence and Paranoia' or *Infinity*, p. 121) or *Zero-Gee Football – It's a Funny Old Game* by Joe Klumpp
   (*Omnibus*, p. 121)
22 Robert Hardy ('Queeg')
23 One thousand and one ('Parallel Universe')
24 The skutters ('Better Than Life')

WORD GRID 1
Insults

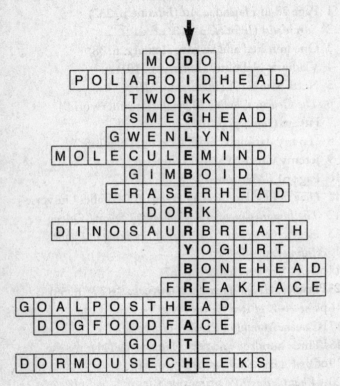

STAIRCASE 2

C	A	D	M	I	U	M
S	A	P	I	E	N	S
G	I	M	B	O	I	D
J	U	P	I	T	E	R
M	A	R	I	L	Y	N
F	L	I	B	B	L	E
J	U	S	T	I	C	E

DIETARY REQUIREMENTS

1 A slice of pizza stolen from a drunken astro (*Infinity*, p. 17)

2 Prawn bangalore phall, half-rice, half-chips, seven spicy poppadoms, a lager-flavoured milkshake and two Rennies (*Infinity*, p. 141)

3 Lightly poached Mimian bladderfish, four-dozen oysters, ducks' feet in abalone sauce, roast suckling pig stuffed with chestnuts and truffles, mashed potatoes with one pint of cream and one pound of butter, gravy and red wine ('Bodyswap')

4 The Indiana Takeaway, St John's Precinct (*Infinity*, p. 150)

5 The lamb ('Better Than Life')

6 Adolf Hitler (and Rimmer) ('Timeslides')

7 That of a spanner ('Thanks for the Memory')

8 Gazpacho soup and chilled champagne ('Me²')

 9 School cabbage ('Marooned' or *BTL*, p. 112)
10 Three pints a night (*Infinity*, p. 57)
11 King prawn (*Infinity*, p. 148)
12 Curry, jam roly-poly and a big jug of margarita ('Out of Time')
13 Keema (*Infinity*, p. 267)
14 Two eggs, three rashers of bacon, a grilled tomato, two sausages, a small portion of fried potatoes and a large quantity of mushrooms ('Stasis Leak')
15 Four (*Infinity*, p. 92)
16 Melly ('Dimension Jump')
17 A dry white wine and Perrier ('Gunmen of the Apocalypse')
18 A half-eaten soya sandwich, a three-quarter-finished noodle burger and the remains of a quintuple-thick milkshake (*Infinity*, p. 37)
19 A week ('Polymorph')
20 Pints of Guinness (*Infinity*, p. 12)
21 Luigi's Fish 'n' Chip Emporium ('Timeslides')
22 Alphabetti spaghetti in tomato sauce, sugar-free baked beans, chicken and mushroom Toastie Toppers and faggots in rich meaty gravy (*Infinity*, p. 123)
23 Dodo pâté (*BTL*, p. 39)
24 A bowl of gazpacho soup (*Infinity*, p. 93)
25 Dehydrated champagne and irradiated caviare niblets (*Infinity*, p. 161)
26 A Christmas pudding flambéed in brandy (*Infinity*, p. 141)
27 A perfect shami kebab (*Infinity*, p. 150)
28 Marzipan (*Infinity*, p. 53)

29 Dom Perignon 1944, in a pint mug ('Better Than
    Life')
30 Prawn ('Future Echoes')
31 A triple fried egg, chilli sauce and chutney sandwich
    ('Thanks for the Memory')
32 A tin of dog food ('Marooned')
33 The 'Lows' ('Demons and Angels')
34 One hundred and thirty (*Infinity*, p. 193)
35 Barium hydrochlorate *salade niçoise*, helium 3 isotopes
    de la maison and a small radioactive fruit salad ('The
    Last Day')
36 Sprout soup, sprout salad, followed by sprout crumble
    ('Quarantine')
37 Lister ('White Hole')
38 'Thicky' Holden ('Timeslides')
39 Olives and water (*BTL*, p. 148)
40 Goat vindaloo ('Balance of Power')
41 Mango juice (Series I – VI)
42 Boiled chicken ovulations ('DNA')
43 Rimmer 2 (*Infinity*, p. 231)
44 Turps ('Out of Time')
45 In the Captain's old donkey jacket ('Legion')
46 Seventy-two ('Balance of Power')
47 Pina coladas (*Infinity*, p. 12)
48 Straight, with ice and lemonade, a cherry and a slice of
    lemon ('Me²'), or straight (*Infinity*, p. 249)
49 A can of last night's flat lager ('Psirens')
50 1799 (*Infinity*, p. 272)
51 Vitamins, goodness and marrowbone jelly ('Kryten' or
    Infinity, p. 174)

52 Dandelion sorbet ('Rimmerworld')
53 Harry Beadlebaum ('Holoship')
54 Double-caffeinated with quadruple sugar ('The Inquisitor')
55 With anti-matter chopsticks ('Legion')
56 The Nice 'n' Noodly Kwik Food Bar (*Infinity*, p. 37)
57 From a book on bacteriological warfare ('Thanks for the Memory')
58 A box of fish paste (*Infinity*, p. 94)
59 Vimto and liquid nitrogen ('The Last Day')
60 A large *quatro formaggio* with extra olives ('Terrorform')
61 Roast beef ('Balance of Power')
62 Bacon and beans ('Emohawk – Polymorph II')
63 Corridor 14: alpha 12 (*Infinity*, p. 76)
64 Sugar puff ('Legion')
65 Four thousand, six hundred and ninety-one ('Balance of Power')
66 Breadman's (*Infinity*, p. 261)
67 In an interlaced log-cabin structure ('Out of Time')
68 Eleven (*Infinity*, p. 110)
69 A colostomy bag ('Polymorph')
70 Dutch lager ('Legion')

CROSSWORD 2

Lister

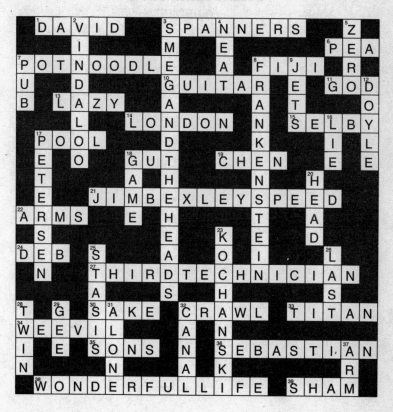

The Red Dwarf Quiz Book

NON-REGISTERED CREW MEMBERS
Byte 2

1 – p	11 – s
2 – j	12 – o
3 – i	13 – r
4 – h	14 – f
5 – n	15 – d
6 – q	16 – m
7 – k	17 – l
8 – a	18 – t
9 – b	19 – g
10 – c	20 – e

JIG WORD 1

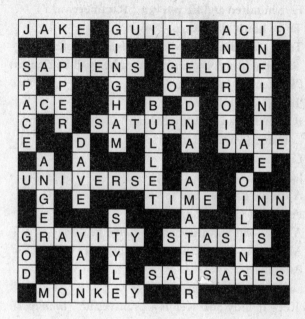

DEEP SMEG!
Megabyte 1

1 Twenty (*Infinity*, p. 117)
2 A star chart leading to the Promised Land ('Waiting for God')
3 Nearly ten years ('Queeg')
4 General George S. Patton's ('The Last Day')
5 Ten: eight women and two men (*Infinity*, p. 161)
6 A tin opener (*Infinity*, p. 123)

7 8.4 ('The Inquisitor')
8 Five hundred and fifty-seven ('Rimmerworld')
9 Three hours (*Infinity*, p. 286)
10 Titan ('The End') or Miranda (*Infinity*, p. 83)
11 'I hope when you come the weather will be clement' ('Kryten' or *Infinity*, p. 170)
12 'Hang' ('Meltdown')
13 Rimmer's dad ('Future Echoes')
14 Lorraine ('Parallel Universe')
15 Liverpool Street (A Monopoly board)
16 John Ewe (*BTL*, p. 127)
17 A couple ('Stasis Leak')
18 Petersen ('Out of Time')
19 A foot-long Havana cigar (*Infinity*, p. 275)
20 All Agatha Christie novels ('Confidence and Paranoia')
21 Snakes ('Polymorph')
22 'Keep It Tidy', or 'Ken Is a Transvestite' (*Infinity*, p. 48)
23 When he is anxious or tense ('Rimmerworld')
24 Mr Spock or Lister ('Bodyswap')
25 His dandruff ('DNA')
26 592 ('Queeg')
27 'The End' and 'Parallel Universe'
28 $£2,000, and it had twenty-five bedrooms (*Infinity*, p. 57)
29 The cats couldn't decide on the colour of the hats in the Hot Dog and Doughnut Diner ('Waiting for God'); or they argued about whether the true Father of Catkind was a man called Cloister or Clister (*Infinity*, p. 124)

30 Lister as the inventor of the Tension Sheet ('Timeslides')

31 Rimmer ('Balance of Power')

32 Six feet five inches ('Better Than Life')

33 Third Console Officer (*Infinity*, p. 69)

34 At the Aigburth Arms, because once he was on the table you couldn't get rid of him ('White Hole' or *BTL*, p. 102)

35 Ten ('Waiting for God')

36 Kinitawowi ('Emohawk – Polymorph II')

37 Don't go and see *Run for your Wife* ('Stasis Leak')

38 Ninety (*Infinity*, p. 75)

39 Seventh Day Advent Hoppists ('The Last Day')

40 Prehistoric World ('Meltdown')

41 White Corridor 159 ('Confidence and Paranoia')

42 Go-Double-Plus (*Infinity*, p. 64)

43 G Deck ('Camille')

44 Stocky ('Holoship')

45 Sidney Poitier and Tony Curtis ('The Inquisitor')

46 Dying ('Rimmerworld')

47 Jimmy Jitterman (*BTL*, p. 58)

48 Rimmer ('Waiting for God')

49 The best part of two thousand years (*Infinity*, p. 124)

50 The Embryo Refrigeration Unit ('Polymorph')

51 Five ('Justice')

52 'Artificial Reality' ('Gunmen of the Apocalypse')

53 Thirteen including Rimmer (*Infinity*, p. 47)

54 Hudzen 10 ('The Last Day')

55 Two hundred and forty-seven ('The End')

56 Rimmer ('Me²')

57 Derek Custer, Kit and Titen ('Rimmerworld')

58 Sigma 14D ('Marooned')

59 In the shower cubicle ('Stasis Leak')

60 10.30 ('Backwards')

61 Executive Officer Carole Brown ('Bodyswap')

62 Because they crashed through an unreality pocket in a reality minefield ('Out of Time')

63 White mink (*Infinity*, p. 264)

64 Anything up to three weeks (*Infinity*, p. 9)

65 Rimmer ('Thanks for the Memory')

66 Twenty-two ('Terrorform')

67 Till the end of the year ('Demons and Angels')

68 One hundred and ninety-eight thousand, seven hundred and thirty-two (*Infinity*, p. 121)

69 Every fourth weekend ('Better Than Life')

70 Grimsby ('Bodyswap')

71 Champion the Wonder Horse ('Kryten' or *Infinity*, p. 171)

72 15.00 hours ('Meltdown')

73 Bay 47 ('Back to Reality')

74 Benny Hill (*Infinity*, p. 287)

75 Fifty-three ('White Hole')

76 They were stoned to death with stale doughnuts ('Waiting for God')

77 Glen Miller ('DNA')

78 Tonto Jitterman (*BTL*, p. 55)

79 Contraceptive jelly ('Me²')

80 In twenty-four hours at 07.00 ('The Last Day')

81 To comb his hair (*Infinity*, p. 92)

82 To have loved and lost ('Stasis Leak')

83 Mimosian ('Legion')

84 Two hundred years ('Psirens')

85 Bay 47 ('Quarantine')
86 Lister (*Infinity*, p. 295)
87 The Spanish (*Infinity*, p. 10)
88 Rimmer ('Out of Time')
89 Thomas Allman ('The Inquisitor')
90 Co-existing realities who share the same space but are unaware of each other's existence ('Dimension Jump')
91 Lister's stepdad's dog ('Future Echoes')
92 Three weeks ('Gunmen of the Apocalypse')
93 Pink neon (*Infinity*, p. 298)
94 A small land mine ('Polymorph')
95 A double lobotomy and ten rolls of rubber wallpaper ('Quarantine')
96 He was hit on the head by a four-thousand-kilogram demolition ball (*Infinity*, p. 27)
97 To conduct the electricity ('Terrorform')
98 It regulates his body temperature ('DNA')
99 2044 ('Thanks for the Memory')
100 Three (*Infinity*, p. 62)
101 The Cat and Lister will choke to death ('Emohawk – Polymorph II')
102 Being put down (*Infinity*, p. 233)
103 One pair to wear on his feet and one to put down the front of his trousers ('Kryten')
104 Nine thousand, three hundred and twenty-eight ('Justice')
105 Experimental pile surgery ('Me²')
106 August, September, September, October, November (*Infinity*, p. 79)
107 Skive hard, play hard ('Balance of Power')
108 To a week last Thursday ('Rimmerworld')

109 The speed of light ('Future Echoes' or *Infinity*, p. 132)
110 'Meltdown' and 'Demons and Angels'
111 The invention of the Steam-Operated Trouser Press (*Infinity*, p. 126)
112 $£50 billion (*BTL*, p. 53)
113 Brannigan ('Queeg')
114 One hundred and fifty ('Justice')
115 Fourteen (*Infinity*, p. 121)
116 St Francis of Assisi ('Holoship')
117 $£8,500 or £18,000 ('Better Than Life')
118 Rimmer ('Parallel Universe')
119 Being on holiday with a group of Germans ('The End')
120 From the vast number of video discs and training films stored in the cargo decks, waiting for delivery to Triton (*Infinity*, p. 127)
121 Sheriff Kryten ('Gunmen of the Apocalypse')
122 A five-day journey (*Infinity*, p. 213)
123 Lieutenant Colonel ('Meltdown')
124 A Yukon bear-trapper on his annual visit to the brothel ('Psirens')
125 Take a photograph (*Infinity*, p. 58)
126 The fifteenth ('Marooned') or fourteenth (*BTL*, p. 110)
127 Lister ('Legion')
128 Twenty-five ('Bodyswap')

WORD SEARCH 2
Baddies!

CLOTHES
(or distraction from the pursuit of intellectual fulfilment)

1. Blue ('Stasis Leak')
2. Two ('Stasis Leak' or *Infinity*, p. 131)
3. Blue (*Infinity*, p. 176)
4. Four years ('Out of Time')
5. Petersen ('Queeg')
6. Sou'westers and asbestos underpants ('The Last Day')
7. Any company in the Burton group (*Infinity*, p. 273)
8. Rimmer ('Rimmerworld')
9. Aquamarine with a diagonal lemon stripe (*Infinity*, p. 44)
10. The Dog ('Parallel Universe')
11. A Spiderman outfit ('Camille')
12. Helen (*BTL*, p. 15)
13. Lister's moon boots ('Kryten')
14. Blue (*Infinity*, p. 71)
15. Kill himself ('Emohawk – Polymorph II')
16. Adrienne (*Infinity*, p. 273)
17. In the air lock ('Kryten')
18. Red, black, white, blue, yellow and orange (*Infinity*, p. 195)
19. 'Me^2' ('Kryten' and 'Better Than Life')
20. Bexley (*Infinity*, p. 270)
21. The one with only two curry stains on it ('Kryten')
22. A sexy black negligée ('Queeg')
23. Robbie Rocket Pants or Junior Birdman ('Terrorform')
24. Three weeks ('Psirens')

WHO SAID THIS, AND WHERE?
Byte 2

1 Rimmer ('The Inquisitor')
2 Lister ('DNA')
3 Rimmer ('Emohawk – Polymorph II')
4 Paranoia ('Confidence and Paranoia')
5 Holly ('Kryten')
6 The Cat ('Thanks for the Memory')
7 Lister ('Emohawk – Polymorph II')
8 Rimmer ('Future Echoes')
9 Hologram Camille ('Camille')
10 The Cat ('Waiting for God')
11 Rimmer ('Parallel Universe')
12 Rimmer ('Confidence and Paranoia')
13 The Cat ('Out of Time')
14 Holly ('The End')
15 Kryten ('Terrorform')
16 The Cat ('White Hole')
17 Rimmer ('Me²')
18 Lister ('Psirens')
19 Rimmer ('Confidence and Paranoia')
20 The Simulant ('Justice')
21 Kryten ('Emohawk – Polymorph II')
22 Lister ('Dimension Jump')
23 Rimmer ('The Last Day')
24 Camille ('Camille')
25 Holly ('Confidence and Paranoia')
26 Kryten ('The Inquisitor')
27 The Cat ('Balance of Power')
28 Rimmer ('Legion')

29 Lister ('The End')
30 The Cat ('Rimmerworld')
31 Kryten ('Terrorform')
32 The Cat ('DNA')
33 Lister ('Waiting for God')
34 Rimmer ('Out of Time')
35 Lister ('Bodyswap')
36 The Cat ('Polymorph')
37 McGruder ('Better Than Life')
38 Rimmer ('Back to Reality')
39 Kryten ('Kryten')
40 Rimmer ('Future Echoes')
41 Lister ('Psirens')
42 The Cat ('White Hole')
43 Kryten ('Gunmen of the Apocalypse')
44 The Polymorph as Rimmer's mum ('Polymorph')
45 Lister ('Back to Reality')

STAIRCASE 3

P	L	A	T	I	N	I
S	A	P	I	E	N	S
M	I	R	R	O	R	S
H	E	R	R	I	N	G
P	O	L	L	O	C	K
R	E	A	L	I	T	Y
D	I	A	R	I	E	S

NUMBER SEARCH

```
3 6 0 0 4 9 4 X 4 R E 1 3 D W 2
9 9 4 1 3 5 3 0 0 6 4 4 2 X 9 0
1 5 9 2 9 N 4 9 1 9 6 4 B 0 2 2
X 0 0 1 8 2 3 5 5 4 1 F 4 1 6 0
4 1 7 2 X 0 Z 4 1 6 7 3 2 W 4 7
B 9 1 7 9 1 2 6 5 B 9 6 9 5 1 7
2 4 7 V 5 4 F 0 8 3 5 0 2 6 8 0
Z X 1 8 0 0 0 3 P 4 3 0 E C 2
i 3 E 5 6 8 9 3 W 6 0 0 0 0 5 3
B 0 3 4 7 A 4 1 5 C 9 4 0 A 0 2
4 3 B 0 5 3 Z 5 4 4 6 2 8 5 0 6
X 5 4 E 9 4 8 2 8 7 4 0 6 1 B 1
2 4 2 0 3 5 B 8 6 9 5 0 X 3 B 6
W 6 7 9 X 7 5 1 5 7 0 7 0 9 2 4
7 i T G 0 0 0 4 9 0 4 5 8 2 3 9
4 7 A 7 9 3 1 0 9 X 5 4 6 8 9 7
3 4 4 5 3 4 0 0 9 2 6 N 4 1 3 0
2 8 1 2 X 2 Y 0 6 0 7 9 8 Z 2
5 7 6 4 0 3 1 0 5 4 0 X 9 C 2 6
9 6 1 0 0 0 6 i W 4 Z 1 3 4 5 1
```

1 000169	9 2X4B	17 2044	25 152
2 E5A908B7	10 1649	18 36	26 4691
3 9328	11 6000	19 14762E	27 592
4 791265B	12 3991	20 4172	28 2/3/2077
5 140000	13 492	21 25	29 47
6 4000GTi	14 12	22 212	30 24A
7 RE13DW	15 ZX81	23 454	31 201
8 8000	16 008	24 27	32 247

SPACE CORPS DIRECTIVES

1 'You have to work in order to earn credits for food' ('Queeg')

2 'No registered vessel should attempt to transverse an asteroid belt without deflectors' ('Psirens')

3 'Demand a re-screening after five days in quarantine' ('Quarantine')

4 'No chance, you metal bastard!' ('White Hole')

5 Space Corps Directive No. 68250 ('Emohawk – Polymorph II')

6 'No officer with false teeth should attempt oral sex in zero gravity' ('Legion')

7 'No member of the Corps should ever report for active duty in a ginger toupee' ('Psirens')

8 'Gross negligence leading to the endangerment of personnel' ('Queeg')

9 'To provide minimum leisure facilities' ('Quarantine')

10 'Any officer caught sniffing the saddle of the exercise bicycle in the women's gym will be discharged without trial' ('Rimmerworld')

11 'One berth per crew member' ('Quarantine')

12 'All nations attending the conference are only allowed one car-parking space' ('Gunmen of the Apocalypse')

JIG WORD 2

DEEP SMEG!
Megabyte 2

1 On 26 February at 8.00 a.m. ('Stasis Leak')
2 Rimmer's Self-Loathing ('Terrorform')
3 The nineteenth ('White Hole')
4 Three hundred and sixty-nine (*Infinity*, p. 75)
5 Lister ('Timeslides')

6 One thousand, one hundred and sixty-seven
  ('Justice')
7 Four minutes and thirty-one seconds ('Queeg')
8 20.36 (*Infinity*, p. 92)
9 Cool, style, grace, *élan* and poise ('Emohawk –
  Polymorph II')
10 Military grey ('Me²')
11 End of conversation ('Balance of Power')
12 Both have been played by David Ross, and they are
   both mechanical ('White Hole')
13 The Fifth Dimension, number six ('Parallel Universe'),
   and The Cartesian Principle, number five (*Infinity*,
   p. 28)
14 With a malfunctioning guidance beam ('Legion')
15 The ninth hole, par four ('Marooned' or *BTL*, p. 113)
16 A chess set with thirty-one missing pieces, a knitting
   magazine with a pull-out special on crocheted hats, a
   puzzle magazine with all the crosswords completed and
   a video of the excellent cinematic treat *Wallpapering,
   Painting and Stippling – A DIY Guide*, plus a looped
   tape of Reggie Dixon's 'Tango Treats' ('Quarantine')
17 Salvador Dali (*Infinity*, p. 7)
18 Arlene Rimmer ('Parallel Universe')
19 Professor Mamet ('Psirens')
20 By turning into a light beam (*BTL*, p. 185)
21 The Odour Eater people ('Thanks for the Memory')
22 $£10 million each (*Infinity*, p. 266)
23 Two stone ('Bodyswap')
24 Macedonia ('Marooned')
25 Five ('White Hole')
26 Triton (*Infinity*, p. 58)

27 George McIntyre ('The End')
28 Rimmer's mum ('Polymorph')
29 Callisto ('The Last Day')
30 Realistic toes and a slide-back sunroof head ('Camille')
31 Mandy's with Candy's (*Infinity*, p. 22)
32 It spreads peace throughout the system, obliterating viral cells as it goes ('Gunmen of the Apocalypse')
33 Four ('Back to Reality')
34 'We are tough, and we are mean – Rimmer's Z Shift get things clean' (*Infinity*, p. 77)
35 Because his physical data disk was corrupted ('Balance of Power')
36 Miss Tracey ('Kryten') or Miss Kirsty (*Infinity*, p. 183)
37 Euston Road and the Angel Islington are the wrong way round (*Infinity*, p. 12)
38 Thirty-four years (*BTL*, p. 163)
39 Drink a pint of his own diarrhoea, or a pint of somebody else's, every hour, on the hour, for the next seventy years (*Infinity*, p. 116)
40 $£1,000 ('The Last Day')
41 Steers and queers ('Meltdown')
42 Five ('Gunmen of the Apocalypse')
43 Fred 'Thicky' Holden ('Timeslides')
44 'Heaven This Way', and her name is tattooed on her bottom (*BTL*, p. 24)
45 Duncan's ('Stasis Leak')
46 His shoes with the compass in the heel and animal tracks on the soles ('Marooned' or *BTL*, p. 114)
47 A Michelangelo statue (*Infinity*, p. 267)
48 Deceitfulness, unpleasantness and offensiveness ('Camille')

The Answers

49 495372 ('Rimmerworld')
50 Pure Mathematics (*Infinity*, p. 17)
51 Because he went into a wine bar ('DNA')
52 'Candy' and 'Denmark forever' ('Balance of Power')
53 A Johnson's baby bud ('Thanks for the Memory')
54 On Thursday ('Polymorph')
55 Three, strawberry (*Infinity*, p. 5)
56 Deganwy ('Queeg')
57 Rameses Niblick III, Kerplunk, Kerplunk, Whoops!, Where's My Thribble? ('White Hole')
58 An android would never rip off a human's head and spit down its neck ('Justice')
59 Three thousand (*Infinity*, p. 259) or three thousand, two hundred and forty-one (*BTL*, p. 11)
60 To refuse an offer of sexual coupling ('Holoship')
61 The good-looking unconventional female journalist ('Legion')
62 Nine thousand, eight hundred per cent (*Infinity*, p. 54)
63 Aliens ('Waiting for God')
64 Rear Admiral Lieutenant General ('Better Than Life')
65 He ventured forth to explore the planet ('Rimmerworld')
66 The Backwards Planet (*BTL*, p. 226)
67 One-fifth ('Me²')
68 'Twenty-four grand' ('Marooned')
69 Death's ('Future Echoes' or *Infinity*, p. 152)
70 Belching 'Yankee Doodle Dandy' ('Parallel Universe')
71 As big as 'King Kong's first dump of the day' ('Psirens')
72 Scorpio and Capricorn (*Infinity*, p. 18)

73 He divorced his parents ('Better Than Life')
74 Whist drive, car-boot sale, street theatre and benefit concerts ('Polymorph' or *BTL*, p. 206)
75 Plastic underpants and a trademark ('The Last Day')
76 In bars on Pheobe, Dione and Rhea (*Infinity*, p. 54)
77 On the inside of a chocolate wrapper ('Balance of Power')
78 When there is only Cinzano left to drink (*BTL*, p. 67)
79 Two years ('Back to Reality')
80 Charles Keelan ('Timeslides')
81 George Washington's (*BTL*, p. 147)
82 Rimmer ('Gunmen of the Apocalypse')
83 20.40 (*Infinity*, p. 93)
84 Forwards ('Out of Time')
85 In Pipeline 22 ('Balance of Power')
86 14 October 2155 (*Infinity*, p. 32)
87 Give him a new body ('Waiting for God')
88 Rimmer was on battery back-up, there was enough oxygen for three months, water for seven weeks, if they drank re-cyc, and two thousand poppadoms ('Psirens')
89 In Lister's pocket ('Stasis Leak')
90 Eighteen months ('The End') or three years (*Infinity*, p. 84)
91 Iron Duke ('Meltdown')
92 Petrovich (*Infinity*, p. 77)
93 Field Marshal Clifton ('Better Than Life')
94 Ten ('Waiting for God')
95 From the highest yard-arm in Titan Docking Port ('Queeg')

96 The man who accidentally got himself attached to
    Lister's group when they first joined *Red Dwarf*
    (*Infinity*, p. 56)

97 From a South African dealer on Callisto (*Infinity*,
    p. 19)

98 His fifth ('The Inquisitor')

99 Four and a half chainsaws ('Legion')

100 A tommy-gun ('Gunmen of the Apocalypse')

101 Floor 14 ('Timeslides')

102 Making sure the vending machines didn't run out of
    fun-size Crunchie bars ('Justice')

103 'Tiger' (*Infinity*, p. 176)

104 Miss Foster ('Queeg')

105 Six months (*Infinity*, p. 14)

106 Hudzen 10 ('The Last Day')

107 Extra rugby practice ('Timeslides')

108 Eco-accelerator rockets ('Rimmerworld')

109 The Goddess of Bar Room Pool (*Infinity*, p. 151)

110 Because he was one inch below regulation height
    ('Better Than Life')

111 Five ('Polymorph')

112 Triton (*Infinity*, p. 58)

113 $£3,000 (*Infinity*, p. 89)

114 Caldicott, his cadet school training officer
    ('Meltdown')

115 Age, rank, seniority and usefulness ('Gunmen of the
    Apocalypse')

116 Turn the crispies into a woman ('Waiting for
    God')

117 Rimmer's dad (*Infinity*, p. 243)

118 The Hitlers ('Out of Time')

119 He stole 'them' from Headbanger Harris ('Stasis Leak')
120 By cable car (*Infinity*, p. 286)
121 'Cowardness, pomposity, snideyness, smarm and basic honest-to-goodness double-dealing two-facedness' ('Rimmerworld')
122 'Bum' ('Justice')
123 Porky Roebuck ('Queeg')
124 Saturn (two hours and ten minutes) (*Infinity*, p. 13)
125 Five or six hundred (*Infinity*, p. 270)
126 Two ('Out of Time')
127 The fact that he is a 'totally worthless, unwashed space bum' ('The Inquisitor')
128 A beautiful alien woman with long green hair and six breasts ('Waiting for God')
129 Love ('Holoship')
130 'Tomorrow is the first day of the rest of your death' (*Infinity*, p. 107)
131 Dr Bob Porkman ('Timeslides')

BACK-ROOM BOYS AND GIRLS

1 Ed Bye
2 'Back to Reality' and 'Quarantine'
3 Bethan Jones
4 Howard Goodall
5 'The Inquisitor'
6 Hilary Bevan Jones

7 Howard Burden
8 'Better Than Life'
9 Peter Wragg
10 Motor City Diva
11 Charles Augins
12 Juliet May
13 Ed Wooden
14 Paul Montague
15 'The Last Day'
16 Paul Jackson
17 Andy De Emmony
18 'Quarantine' and 'Rimmerworld'
19 Lighting Director
20 Graham Hutchings
21 'Balance of Power', 'Future Echoes' and 'Me²'
22 Jill Dornan
23 Dave Fox
24 Kerry Waddell
25 Karl Mooney
26 Graphic Designer
27 Mario Dubois
28 'Back to Reality'
29 Suzannah Holt
30 Stunt Co-ordinator

STAIRCASE 4

```
M I R A N D A
C A P T A I N
G A R B A G E
J U P I T E R
C A M I L L E
M O N K E Y S
P O R K M A N
```

'CAN YOU SEE THAT SPACE VEHICLE?'

1 To write 'Coke Adds Life!' in stars (*Infinity*, p. 162)
2 *Starbug* 1 (or *Starbug* 2) ('Backwards')
3 *Pax Vert* (*Infinity* p. 57)
4 Four thousand ('Future Echoes')
5 Three miles wide, four miles deep and nearly six miles long (*Infinity*, p. 49)
6 SCS *Pioneer* ('Psirens')
7 Demi–light speed Zippers (*Infinity*, p. 62)
8 In the middle of the Sahara desert (*Infinity*, p. 261)
9 A 'sardine tin' ('Back to Reality')
10 Quadrant 4, Sector 492 ('Holoship')
11 Sixty (*Infinity* p. 186)
12 A ZX81 ('Psirens')
13 Mimas, Saturn ('Dimension Jump')
14 Two hundred thousand miles per hour (*Infinity* p. 131)

15 The *Arthur C. Clarke* (*Infinity*, p. 38)
16 A matter of nano-seconds ('Legion')
17 'To introduce oceanic life to potential S3 planets,
    recon trip, three-year check, strictly routine, to make
    sure the amino-acid chain had taken' ('Back to
    Reality')
18 Shuttle Flight JMC159 for *White Giant* (*Infinity*, p. 35)
19 A metre-thick strontium/agol alloy (*Infinity*, p. 195)
20 The left one ('Psirens')
21 Four years and three months ('Backwards')
22 $£800 (*Infinity*, p. 14)
23 A planet with the right atmosphere for a garden
    ('Kryten')

WORD SEARCH 3
Cosmic!

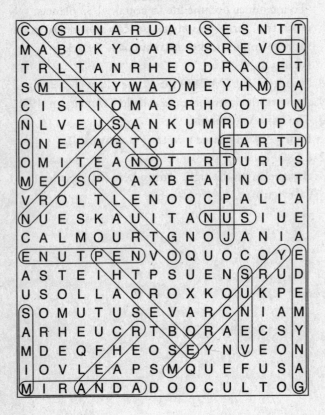

NON-REGISTERED CREW MEMBERS
Byte 3

1 – m	11 – o
2 – j	12 – t
3 – q	13 – h
4 – s	14 – e
5 – i	15 – k
6 – r	16 – l
7 – a	17 – g
8 – c	18 – n
9 – p	19 – f
10 – b	20 – d

CROSSWORD 3

Holly

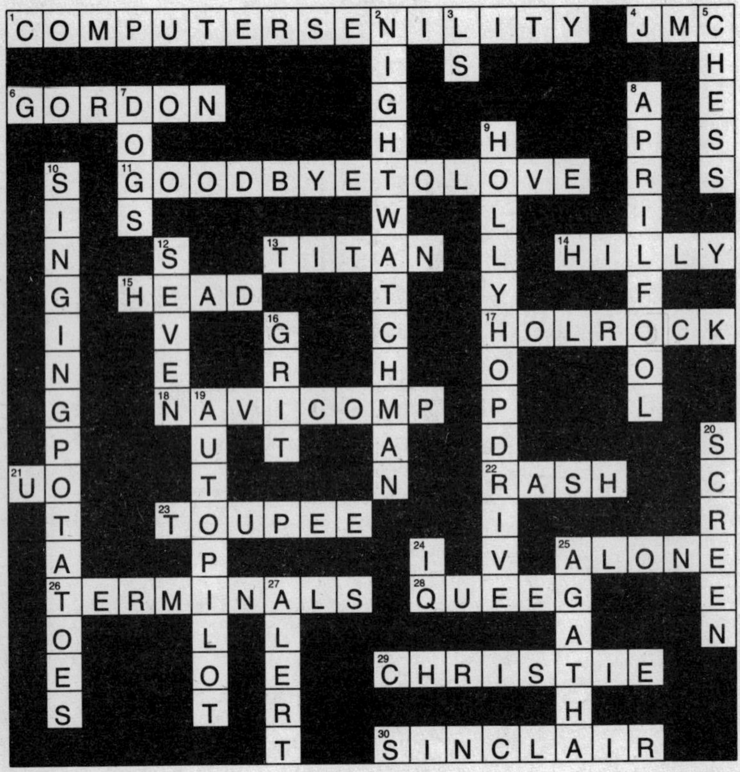
1 COMPUTERSENILITY
4 JMC
6 GORDON
11 GOODBYETOLOVE
13 TITAN
14 HILLY
15 HEAD
17 HOLROCK
18 NAVICOMP
21 UO
22 RASH
23 TOUPEE
25 ALONE
26 TERMINALS
28 QUEEG
29 CHRISTIE
30 SINCLAIR
2 NIGHTWATCHMAN
3 LS
5 CHESS
7 DOGS
8 APRILFOOL
9 HOLLYHOPDRIVE
10 SINGINGPOTATOES
12 SEVEN
16 GRIT
19 AUTOPILOT
20 SCREEN
24 I
25 AGATHA
27 ALERT

WORD GRID 2
Space sickness

```
            S P A C E M U M P S
        C O M P U T E R R A S H
        D I A R R H O E A
            D E L I R I U M
          B R O K E N L E G S
      I N D I G E S T I O N
            P R E G N A N C Y
    C O M P U T E R S E N I L I T Y
      D A N D R U F F
          D R O I D R O T
        H O L O V I R U S
        D E A T H
```

OH SMEG INDEED, MATEY!
Megabyte 1

1 Enough to illuminate Paris for three years (*Infinity*, p. 29)
2 Console Executive Imran Sanchez (*Infinity*, p. 99)
3 One hundred and seventy-three ('Balance of Power')
4 His Engineering finals (*Infinity*, p. 205)
5 A vacuum cleaner, buzz saw, power drill, hedge trimmer and an egg whisk ('Polymorph')

6 Twelve (*Infinity*, p. 47)
7 The Louvre ('DNA')
8 Saxon and Burroughs (*Infinity*, p. 76)
9 One hour, seventeen minutes and thirty-nine seconds ('Emohawk – Polymorph II')
10 Fifteen out of eighty-four (*Infinity*, p. 230)
11 At Saturn Tech. ('Thanks for the Memory')
12 Floor 9172, Area P (*Infinity*, p. 44)
13 A Dutch astro called 'Dutch' (*BTL*, p. 52)
14 The Mayor of Warsaw ('Confidence and Paranoia')
15 Miss Elaine (*Infinity*, p. 183)
16 Two thousand, five hundred and sixty-seven ('Stasis Leak')
17 Petrovich's (*Infinity*, p. 79)
18 356 by 121 ('Emohawk – Polymorph II')
19 Five thousand, five hundred and twenty-five to one ('Quarantine')
20 The Happy Astro (*Infinity*, p. 64)
21 Donald ('Marooned')
22 Five hundred ('Waiting for God')
23 Because he left a light on in his bathroom before joining up ('Me²')
24 On the island of Zanzibar (*BTL*, p. 174)
25 Legion's ('Legion')
26 The crew to turn into 'ice-skating mongooses and dance the Bolero' ('Gunmen of the Apocalypse')
27 Non-fissile thorium isotope: thorium 232 (*Infinity*, p. 213)
28 Kryten ('Rimmerworld')
29 No. 1344 (*Infinity*, p. 93)
30 Four ('Holoship')

31 A skutter ('Confidence and Paranoia')
32 The service robots ('The End')
33 Saturn (*Infinity*, p. 4)
34 Floor 592 ('Queeg')
35 Herman Munster's ('Legion')
36 One month (*Infinity*, p. 18)
37 A pair of wellingtons ('Future Echoes')
38 'Last Thursday' ('Gunmen of the Apocalypse')
39 Alison Bredbury (*Infinity*, p. 177)
40 Forty-seven ('Holoship')
41 He reversed over his Aunt Belinda's show poodle (*BTL*, p. 95)
42 A man who works for the Post Office ('Confidence and Paranoia')
43 The barmaid in the Last Chance Saloon ('Gunmen of the Apocalypse')
44 Rimmer ('Out of Time')
45 Two hours ('Quarantine')
46 The Eastbourne Zimmerframe Relay Team ('Emohawk – Polymorph II')
47 1952 ('Camille')
48 To prolong the torment of their torture victims ('Rimmerworld')
49 Forty-five minutes (*Infinity*, p. 234)
50 Elaine Salinger (*BTL*, p. 146)
51 Behind the solar panel outside the sleeping quarters ('Confidence and Paranoia')
52 The 'man with the dirty mac who discovered America' ('Waiting for God')
53 Sixty billion miles ('Better Than Life')
54 Mercury ('Legion')

55 Over two thousand ('Bodyswap')
56 In 2230 – fifty years' time (Lister was born in 2155; he was twenty-five years old when he signed up – i.e. in 2180; then add fifty years) (*Infinity*, p. 18)
57 Having formed the 'Valkyrie Sex-Slave Liberation Movement', they left for the mainland (*BTL*, p. 75)
58 Eighteen hours ('Confidence and Paranoia')
59 Bull Heinman (*BTL*, p. 54)
60 Heavy metal ('Timeslides')
61 Two hundred thousand ('Holoship')
62 'KIT, or Paint Before Assembling' ('Out of Time')
63 Kryten 2X4B 523P ('The Last Day')
64 Fifty-three ('Emohawk – Polymorph II')
65 Two hundred thousand light years ('Meltdown')
66 It stimulates the dormant psychic areas of the brain ('Quarantine')
67 To have a little cry in the corner ('Me²')
68 The Bahamas (*Infinity*, p. 265)
69 Ten (*BTL*, p. 131)
70 Six hundred ('Rimmerworld')
71 Confidence ('Confidence and Paranoia')
72 The Cat ('Emohawk – Polymorph II')
73 Kryten ('Legion')
74 Five ('Demons and Angels')
75 He hitched a ride in a frozen-meat truck (*Infinity*, p. 12)
76 Prussian blue on a yellow ochre background (*Infinity*, p. 65)
77 He hummed ('Me²')
78 Marie Antoinette, Josephine Bonaparte, Imelda Marcos and Liz Taylor (*BTL*, p. 53)
79 Rimmer's lift attendant (*Infinity*, p. 264)

80 Kryten ('Out of Time')

81 *Butch Accountant and the Yuppie Kid* ('Gunmen of the Apocalypse')

82 00110011101110001111001110011100 ('Terrorform')

83 Fourteen months (*Infinity*, p. 265)

84 Jean-Paul Sartre ('Balance of Power' or *Infinity*, p. 105)

85 When he was Duane Dibbley ('Emohawk – Polymorph II')

86 Seventeen ('Confidence and Paranoia')

87 Perverse pleasure ('Emohawk – Polymorph II')

88 Mr Mulligan (*BTL*, p. 8)

89 Red-hot West Indian red pepper sauce ('Rimmerworld')

90 There wasn't one ('Thanks for the Memory')

91 His right one, replaced by a telephoto lens (*Infinity*, p. 157)

92 Captain Hollister ('Thanks for the Memory'), Lister ('Bodyswap') and Goering ('Meltdown')

93 Mr Calhoon (*Infinity*, p. 285)

94 Lister ('Confidence and Paranoia')

95 His disappointment and his Javanese camphor-wood trunk ('Marooned')

96 Every Tuesday (*Infinity*, p. 193)

97 Rimmer ('Me²')

98 Lister's socks ('Polymorph')

99 The E string of his guitar ('The End')

100 Julius Caesar (*Infinity*, p. 107)

101 Junior D ('Dimension Jump')

102 Partnership whist ('Psirens')

103 Five ('The Inquisitor')

104 Two thousand, five hundred and seventy-two (*Infinity*, p. 210)

105 Because Lister came bottom in French ('Future Echoes')

106 Science Officer Buchan, IQ 169, and Flight Co-ordinator McQueen, IQ 172 ('Holoship')

107 For talking at lunch and snoring with malicious intent (*BTL*, p. 203)

108 Old Mrs Davis (*Infinity*, p. 240)

STAIRCASE 5

L	E	N	N	O	N
M	I	L	L	E	R
F	I	S	H	E	R
K	R	Y	T	E	N
R	A	C	H	E	L
H	I	T	L	E	R

CROSSWORD 4

The Cat

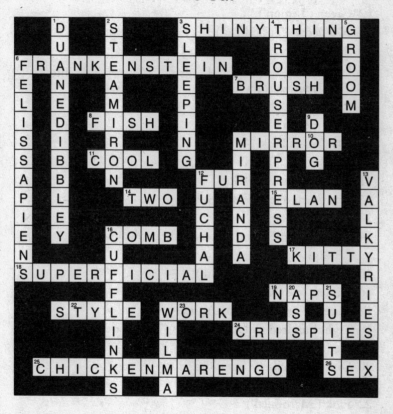

OBSERVATION DOME

1 *Red Dwarf* – ship's issue ('Polymorph')
2 Green ('Legion')
3 *Newsweek* ('Timeslides')
4 'Home Sweet Home' ('Stasis Leak')
5 F (Series I and II)
6 The Titan Hilton ('Confidence and Paranoia')
7 'Backwards'
8 'Polymorph'
9 008 ('Stasis Leak')
10 Jim Reaper ('The Last Day')
11 Red ('Waiting for God')
12 The green one ('White Hole')
13 Fourteen ('Legion')
14 When he stole Lister's body and ran away with it ('Bodyswap')
15 The Welsh flag ('The End')
16 His left one ('Dimension Jump')
17 Three ('Gunmen of the Apocalypse')
18 Eight hundred and seventy-one ('Backwards')
19 Red ('The End')
20 Don Donatella ('Timeslides')
21 Rimmer's mum ('Polymorph')
22 Pink ('Marooned')
23 *Muscle Woman* ('Bodyswap')
24 Red tartan ('Stasis Leak')
25 Kryten ('Terrorform')
26 Three ('Quarantine')
27 'DNA', 'The Inquisitor', 'Demons and Angels', 'Legion', 'Rimmerworld' and 'Out of Time'

28 'Dimension Jump' (according to the original transmission of the series)
29 On Captain Hollister's desk ('The End')
30 *Nivelo* ('The End')
31 Red ('Future Echoes')
32 A yellow toy car (shown in a photograph in 'Timeslides')
33 A hamster ('DNA')
34 Heliotrope ('Terrorform')
35 Red ('Back to Reality')
36 Cinelli ('Parallel Universe')
37 Level 454 ('The End')
38 Z ('Confidence and Paranoia')
39 *Kinejo* ('Me²')
40 Twenty-five ('Kryten')
41 Channel 27 ('Better Than Life')
42 Domestos ('Bodyswap')
43 The left one ('Justice')
44 152 ('Quarantine')
45 A tyrannosaurus, fish, dolphin, duck, eagle, rabbit, cow, lion, penguin, woman, pig and man ('Psirens')
46 1875 ('Gunmen of the Apocalypse')
47 Numbers 1 or 2 (Series III onwards)
48 Kylie Gwenlyn ('Kryten')
49 882 FOP ('Better Than Life')
50 Tetley's bitter ('Backwards')
51 Seven ('Marooned')
52 On a postcard beside Lister's bunk ('Bodyswap')
53 Machine No. 16 ('Back to Reality')
54 On her right cheekbone and the left-hand side of her chin ('Gunmen of the Apocalypse')

55 Unit No. 8 ('Emohawk – Polymorph II')
56 Harley Davidson, C222 PFY ('Better Than Life')
57 Marilyn Monroe ('Better Than Life')
58 The Cat's right leg and Lister's left ('Thanks for the Memory')
59 When he took out Lister's willy for a wee when he swapped bodies with him ('Bodyswap')
60 Two ('Demons and Angels')
61 Blue ('Legion')
62 1736 ('Rimmerworld')
63 Maintenance Personnel ('Better Than Life')
64 Red ('Future Echoes')
65 It is in the middle (Series III onwards)
66 129 and 4457 ('Future Echoes')
67 Tennent's Super ('Thanks for the Memory')
68 Beside his bunk ('Camille')
69 Six hundred ('Demons and Angels')
70 'Cigarettes and whisky and wild, wild women' ('Gunmen of the Apocalypse')
71 Wednesday 2 March 2077, at 8.30 ('Stasis Leak')
72 A female skutter ('Parallel Universe')
73 The Union Jack and the Stars and Stripes ('Waiting for God')
74 A banana ('Camille')
75 The Streets of Laredo ('Gunmen of the Apocalypse')
76 The Cat – a stag; Lister – a wolf; Kryten – a chicken; and Rimmer – a fox ('Out of Time')
77 *My Incredible Career* ('Better Than Life')
78 In the shower cubicle ('Stasis Leak')
79 It had fish in it ('Parallel Universe')
80 *The Times* ('Me²')

The Answers

81 Brooke Junior ('Kryten')
82 Chaz ('Marooned')
83 A slug-like monster, teddy, bucket and spade, pot plant, toy truck, flamenco doll, telephone, elephant, top hat, baseball glove and ball, boxer Action Man, toy drum, flashing beacon, toy Volkswagen, roller skate, traffic cone, lampshade, inflatable penguin, pig, Ken doll, potty, alarm clock, ball, trainer, saucepan, pom-pom, scrubbing brush, metal pail, dolphin, statue, light bulb, air horn, ball, sock, rabbit, basketball, shami kebab diabolo, boxer shorts, large snake, eight-foot-tall armour-plated killing machine, large splodgy squelchy thing, woman, Rimmer, a slug in the tap, Bonehead's mum and Lister (phew!) ('Polymorph')
84 Leopard ('DNA')
85 His right one ('White Hole')
86 The left ('Demons and Angels')
87 By grasping each other's right ankle ('Emohawk – Polymorph II')
88 Unit No. 8 ('Out of Time')
89 Blue and cream ('Parallel Universe')
90 791265/B ('Kryten')
91 Moët et Chandon ('Stasis Leak')
92 Red ('Demons and Angels')
93 Laxo ('Better Than Life')
94 Green ('Emohawk – Polymorph II')
95 *Red Dwarf*, Deep Space, RE1 3DW ('Better Than Life')
96 Lister's hat, a chicken, large tin of baked beans, frog, paper plane, microphone, spring, remote-control buggy car, thermos, Emohawk, a grenade and Emohawk again ('Emohawk – Polymorph II')

97 A male skutter ('Parallel Universe')
98 His right one ('Demons and Angels')
99 Rimmer ('Emohawk – Polymorph II')

JIG WORD 3

MINIMUM LEISURE FACILITIES

1 Haydn's Surprise Symphony (*BTL*, p. 43)
2 Johnny Cologne (*Infinity*, p. 58)

3 Myra Binglebat and Peter Beardsley ('Better Than Life')

4 Frank Capra's *It's a Wonderful Life* (*Infinity*, p. 69)

5 Peter Perfect ('Demons and Angels')

6 *Gone with the Wind* ('Stasis Leak')

7 Hugo Lovepole (*Infinity*, p. 211)

8 *God, I Love this War!* (*Infinity*, p. 50)

9 'See Ya Later, Alligator' ('The End')

10 Copacabana ('Terrorform')

11 *The Wild One, Easy Rider,* and *Rebel Without a Cause* ('Kryten')

12 'Goodbye to Love' ('Queeg')

13 His left one ('DNA')

14 Rasta Billy Skank ('Balance of Power')

15 Total Immersion Video Games ('Better Than Life')

16 'She's out of my Life' ('Marooned')

17 Jimi Hendrix (*Infinity*, p. 291)

18 Wednesday ('Dimension Jump')

19 Reggie Dixon ('Quarantine')

20 Quartet for Nine Players in H Sharp Minor (*Infinity*, p. 169)

21 Hoagy Carmichael (*BTL*, p. 39)

22 Leisure World International ('Back to Reality')

23 *The Flintstones* (*Infinity*, p. 119)

24 Doug McClure's ('Legion')

25 Julius Caesar (*Infinity*, p. 274)

26 1649 ('Better Than Life')

27 A can of Jiffy Windo-Kleen (*Infinity*, p. 182)

28 'Born to Brutalize' (*BTL*, p. 217)

29 Zero-Gee football (Series I onwards)

30 Doh, ray, me, fah, soh, lah, woh, boh, ti, doh ('Kryten' or *Infinity*, p. 168)

31 Late at night ('Legion')
32 One thousand, nine hundred and seventy-four (*Infinity*, p. 182)
33 'Fly Me to the Moon' ('Future Echoes')
34 *Nice 'n' Nauseating* (*Infinity*, p. 38)
35 Mantovani ('Thanks for the Memory')
36 Gordon ('Better Than Life')
37 On Friday nights (*Infinity*, p. 181)
38 Gordon ('Better Than Life') or Queeg ('Queeg')
39 Three million ('Timeslides')
40 Lister ('Confidence and Paranoia')

WORD SEARCH 4

The Rimmers

WHO SAID THIS, AND WHERE?
Byte 3

1 Rimmer ('Thanks for the Memory')
2 Lister ('Quarantine')
3 The Cat ('Confidence and Paranoia')
4 Kryten ('Out of Time')
5 Rimmer ('The Inquisitor')
6 Elvis Presley ('Meltdown')
7 Lister ('Quarantine')
8 Rimmer ('Kryten')
9 Holly ('Queeg')
10 The Cat ('Demons and Angels')
11 The Male Simulant ('Gunmen of the Apocalypse')
12 Lister ('Balance of Power')
13 Rimmer ('Parallel Universe')
14 Holly ('Thanks for the Memory')
15 The Cat ('Better Than Life')
16 Lister ('Bodyswap')
17 Rimmer ('Gunmen of the Apocalypse')
18 Kryten ('Psirens')
19 Holly ('Future Echoes')
20 Lister's Gelf bride ('Emohawk – Polymorph II')
21 Rimmer ('Polymorph')
22 Lister ('Terrorform')
23 The Cat ('Meltdown')
24 Kryten ('Kryten')
25 The Cat ('Legion')
26 Rimmer ('Confidence and Paranoia')
27 Rimmer ('Out of Time')
28 The Cat ('Rimmerworld')

29 Dr Lanstrom ('Quarantine')
30 Lister ('Psirens')
31 Lister ('Polymorph')
32 The Cat ('Me²')
33 Ace Rimmer ('Dimension Jump')
34 Kryten ('White Hole')
35 The Cat ('The Inquisitor')
36 Rimmer ('Rimmerworld')
37 Rimmer ('Balance of Power')
38 The Cat ('Legion')
39 Kryten ('Justice')
40 Rimmer ('Waiting for God')
41 The Cat ('Justice')
42 Lister ('Out of Time')
43 Rimmer ('Back to Reality')
44 The Cat ('Polymorph')
45 Kryten ('Psirens')
46 Nirvanah Crane ('Holoship')

OH SMEG INDEED, MATEY!
Megabyte 2

1 'Pinkle, squirmy, plip plap plop!' ('Queeg')
2 Twenty-four (*Infinity*, p. 76)
3 He scrunches them up and throws them in the bin ('Out of Time')
4 'Truth' and 'Agony' ('Demons and Angels')
5 'Special Weapons and Tactics Unit' (*BTL*, p. 68)

6 Lister's hidden cigarettes ('Balance of Power')
7 T'ai-Ch'ang, also known as Chu Ch'ang-lo Kuang
   Tsung (*Infinity*, p. 44)
8 One of Lister's sneezes ('Legion')
9 Caltech (*Infinity*, p. 194)
10 The President of Callisto (*BTL*, p. 131)
11 The laboratory mice ('The End')
12 Six months ('White Hole')
13 Floor 3125 ('Holoship')
14 In a Photo-U-Kwik booth (*Infinity*, p. 57)
15 With an F ('Legion')
16 Tetchy ('Quarantine')
17 Page 47 ('White Hole')
18 Malnutrition ('Better Than Life')
19 Sidcup (*Infinity*, p. 27)
20 Taiwan ('Out of Time')
21 Eleven ('Waiting for God')
22 'Sonic super mop' (*Infinity*, p. 49)
23 Rimmer's cheque book (*Infinity*, p. 275)
24 A hundred-and-fifty-second and third (*Infinity*, p. 11)
25 On her bottom (*Infinity*, p. 269)
26 010101 ('Bodyswap')
27 Twelve ('DNA')
28 Clark Gable (*Infinity*, p. 282)
29 27 October (*Infinity*, p. 79)
30 The tin opener ('Out of Time')
31 Five million ('Back to Reality')
32 The pile of laundry in the washroom ('Psirens')
33 Chelsea Brown (*Infinity*, p. 111)
34 Three feet ('The End')
35 The Berlin Bandits (*Infinity*, p. 150)

36 An Italian waiter's keks ('Marooned')

37 Execution ('Emohawk – Polymorph II')

38 Cell 41 (*BTL*, p. 54)

39 6.47 minutes ('Future Echoes')

40 13 January (*Infinity*, p. 168)

41 In another couple of ice ages ('Justice')

42 The cooking tongs ('Out of Time')

43 Machine 15455 (*Infinity*, p. 76)

44 Frank ('Future Echoes') or Christopher (*Infinity*, p. 25)

45 The Total Immersion Video Game 'Better Than Life' ('Better Than Life')

46 Fifty-eight ('Timeslides')

47 Thirty-two including Legion ('Legion')

48 A Nantucket fisherman (*BTL*, p. 37)

49 Kochanski ('Balance of Power')

50 Kochanski's remains (*BTL*, p. 226)

51 Pages 25–59 ('Queeg')

52 579 Automatic 14F stop cornea ('Camille')

53 Trapped (*Infinity*, p. 127)

54 One hundred and forty-seven (*Infinity*, p. 149)

55 For his diligence and general devotion to duty ('The End')

56 To pedal for the electric blanket ('White Hole')

57 'A couple of hundred thousand years max' (*Infinity*, p. 102)

58 Eight years ('Kryten' or *Infinity*, p. 171)

59 A pan-dimensional liquid beast from the Mogadon cluster ('Out of Time')

60 The Captain's formal dinner (*Infinity*, p. 251)

61 Five ('Waiting for God')

62 Three ('Confidence and Paranoia')

63 The woman who Rimmer said had got run over by a bus and wanted a cure for her death (*Infinity*, p. 113)

64 The tenth (*Infinity*, p. 153)

65 One (*Infinity*, p. 247)

66 A super-de-luxe vacuum cleaner, triple bag, easy-glide vac with turbo-vac and a self-emptying dust bag ('DNA')

67 In the Austrian town of Salzburg, when a vacuum cleaner and Gelf Volkswagen Beetle robbed a high-street bank. They took the manager and a security guard hostage, agreeing to release them only if Valter Holman was brought to justice for murder (*BTL*, p. 173)

68 A Bentley convertible V8 turbo ('Marooned' or *BTL*, p. 113)

69 Lister ('Rimmerworld')

70 Henry LeClerk ('Better Than Life')

71 The 345 ('Quarantine')

72 11.45 (*Infinity*, p. 86)

73 Dispenser 172 ('The End')

74 Lister ('Bodyswap')

75 Aries ('Emohawk – Polymorph II')

76 Pop Buckley (*BTL*, p. 23)

77 Rimmer 1 (*Infinity*, p. 220)

78 Tightly packed particles from an exploded super nova ('Out of Time')

79 Set about him with a petrol-powered chainsaw (*BTL*, p. 177)

80 Four (*Infinity*, p. 73)

81 1 February ('White Hole')

82 McWilliams ('Marooned')

83 The theory of relativity ('Future Echoes')
84 Their hair-dryers were confiscated and they were forced to wear fashions some two or three seasons old (*Infinity*, p. 128)
85 By skating ('Balance of Power')
86 'Genetic Alternative Sports' (*BTL*, p. 172)
87 At 9.00 p.m. (*Infinity*, p. 181)
88 He's disciplined, organized, dedicated to his career, and he's always got a pen ('Thanks for the Memory')
89 On Corridor 4: delta 799 (*Infinity*, p. 85)
90 Daddy ('Confidence and Paranoia')
91 Ten (*Infinity*, p. 233)
92 The Hi-Life Club (*Infinity*, p. 210)
93 Hamstergrams ('Camille')
94 It had 'two hundred needle-sharp silver teeth' (*BTL*, p. 191)
95 Alice and Sarah ('The Last Day')
96 His left one ('Bodyswap')
97 Forty minutes (*Infinity*, p. 182)
98 A photograph of Rimmer's mum ('Me²')
99 9.00 p.m (*Infinity*, p. 224)
100 Jupiter rise ('Future Echoes')
101 Barbara (*Infinity*, p. 69)
102 Roze (*Infinity*, p. 182)
103 Three days ('Out of Time')
104 Three minutes (*Infinity*, p. 127)
105 Talkie Toaster (*BTL*, p. 225)
106 In the skutters' broom cupboard ('Better Than Life')

CROSSWORD 5
Kryten

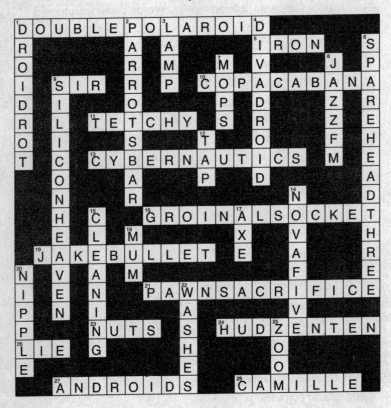

NON-REGISTERED CREW MEMBERS
Byte 4

1 – g	11 – n
2 – f	12 – a
3 – k	13 – r
4 – i	14 – p
5 – t	15 – s
6 – h	16 – o
7 – d	17 – c
8 – m	18 – b
9 – e	19 – l
10 – q	20 – j

WORD SEARCH 5

Famous people

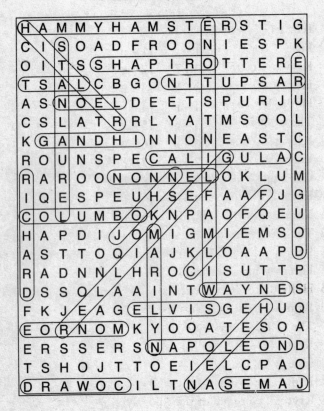

```
H A M M Y H A M S T E R S T I G
C I S O A D F R O O N I E S P K
O I T S S H A P I R O T T E R E
T S A L C B G O N I T U P S A R
A S N O E L D E E T S P U R J U
C S L A T R R L Y A T M S O O L
K G A N D H I N N O N E A S T C
R O U N S P E C A L I G U L A C
R A R O O N O N N E L O K L U M
I Q E S P E U H S E F A A F J G
C O L U M B O K N P A O F Q E U
H A P D I J O M I G M I E M S O
A S T T O Q I A J K L O A A P D
R A D N N L H R O C I S U T T P
D S S O L A A I N T W A Y N E S
F K J E A G E L V I S G E H U Q
E O R N O M K Y O O A T E S O A
E R S S E R S N A P O L E O N D
T S H O J T T O E I E L C P A O
D R A W O C I L T N A S E M A J
```

WHO SAID THIS, AND WHERE?
Byte 4

1 Rimmer ('Better Than Life')
2 Lister ('Back to Reality')
3 Kryten ('Justice')
4 Lister ('Thanks for the Memory')
5 Holly ('Queeg')
6 The Cat ('Psirens')
7 Rimmer ('Timeslides')
8 Lister ('DNA')
9 Confidence ('Confidence and Paranoia')
10 Kryten ('Rimmerworld')
11 Thomas Allman ('The Inquisitor')
12 The Cat ('Future Echoes')
13 Rimmer (as Brannigan) ('Queeg')
14 Lister ('Rimmerworld')
15 Holly ('Future Echoes')
16 Rimmer ('Parallel Universe')
17 The Cat ('Meltdown')
18 Kryten ('Meltdown')
19 Lister ('Legion')
20 Rimmer ('Dimension Jump')
21 Kryten ('Gunmen of the Apocalypse')
22 McIntyre ('The End')
23 Holly ('Terrorform')
24 Rimmer ('Emohawk – Polymorph II')
25 The Cat ('Stasis Leak')
26 Petersen ('Stasis Leak')
27 Kryten ('Rimmerworld')
28 The Cat ('Psirens')

29 Rimmer ('Terrorform')
30 Melly ('Dimension Jump')
31 The Cat ('Balance of Power')
32 Kryten ('Quarantine')
33 Rimmer ('Confidence and Paranoia')
34 Holly ('Queeg')
35 Kryten ('Psirens')
36 Rimmer ('Better Than Life')
37 The Cat ('Rimmerworld')
38 Rimmer ('Quarantine')
39 Death Apocalypse ('Gunmen of the Apocalypse')
40 The Cat ('Waiting for God')
41 Rimmer ('Out of Time')
42 The Cat ('Out of Time')
43 Ace Rimmer ('Emohawk – Polymorph II')
44 Lister ('Psirens')
45 Paranoia ('Confidence and Paranoia')
46 Kryten ('Psirens')

STAIRCASE 6

A	L	B	E	R	T
G	R	O	O	V	Y
D	U	N	C	A	N
A	W	O	O	G	A
P	A	D	D	L	E
I	N	G	R	I	D

GIRLS FROM THE *DWARF*

1 Carole (*Infinity*, p. 4)
2 Carol McCauley ('Stasis Leak')
3 Susan Warrington ('Marooned') or Michelle Fisher (*BTL*, p. 113)
4 Fiona Barrington ('The Inquisitor')
5 E5A908B7 ('Camille')
6 Lorraine ('Parallel Universe')
7 Lise Yates ('Thanks for the Memory')
8 A Sinclair ZX81 ('Stasis Leak')
9 Sandra ('Marooned' or *BTL*, p. 113)
10 'Heartbreakers and moral garbage on legs' ('Gunmen of the Apocalypse')
11 Helen (*BTL*, p. 15)
12 Norman ('Confidence and Paranoia') or Alan (*BTL*, p. 112)
13 Lady Sabrina Mulholland-Jjones ('Timeslides')
14 Rimmer's polythene pal ('Queeg')
15 Ida Lupino (*Infinity*, p. 286)
16 His Uncle Frank ('The Last Day')
17 His sister-in-law, Janine ('Camille')
18 Melly ('Dimension Jump')
19 Frank 'The Enforcer' Nitty's girlfriend (*BTL*, p. 4)
20 Seven, and one on the way ('Better Than Life')
21 Peter Tranter's sister ('Psirens')
22 Loretta ('Gunmen of the Apocalypse')
23 Louis XVI's ('Out of Time')
24 Wilma Flintstone ('Backwards' or *BTL*, p. 97)
25 Nirvanah Crane ('Holoship')
26 Frank Rimmer (*BTL*, p. 29)

27 Twelve minutes (7.31 – 7.43), on 16 March ('Thanks for the Memory')
28 Camille ('Camille')
29 Sarah ('The Last Day')

WORD SEARCH 6
Animals from the Dwarf

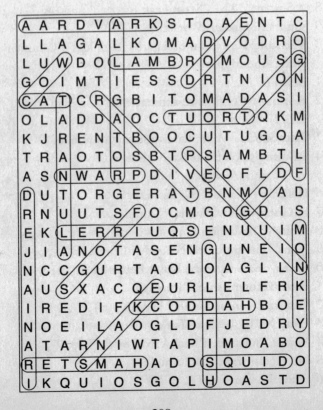

OH SMEG INDEED, MATEY!
Megabyte 3

1 That love is a sickness that holds back your career and makes you spend all your money ('Confidence and Paranoia')
2 In the Sea of Tranquility (*Infinity*, p. 18)
3 The tallest of the Valkyries (*Infinity*, p. 289)
4 John F. Kennedy, Vincent Van Gogh, Albert Einstein, Louis XVI and Elvis Presley (*BTL*, p. 3)
5 As 'young' Lister, when Rimmer told him the 'Om' song was good ('Timeslides')
6 The lamp ('The Last Day')
7 The entire military budget of the USA for the whole of history (*Infinity*, p. 162)
8 A skin-diving suit with the bottom cut out (*BTL*, p. 15)
9 Because Kochanski had finished with him ('DNA')
10 'A-line flares with pockets in the knees' ('Legion')
11 A 14F ('The End')
12 'Old Tobacco Boots' (*Infinity*, p. 76)
13 A Chinese restaurant (*Infinity*, p. 252)
14 Because he hadn't mowed the lawn (*BTL*, p. 203)
15 Total Immersion Video Games ('Better Than Life')
16 Not a single creature, but a combination of individuals melded together to form one ('Legion' or Grant Naylor!)
17 'No, you're a filthy, stinking, loathsome, disgusting object. I wouldn't be seen dead with you in a plague pit' ('Confidence and Paranoia')
18 The universe (*Infinity*, p. 167)

19 Soap, deodorant and socks ('The End')
20 Ninety-one per cent ('The Last Day')
21 Noisily evacuate their waste fumes (*BTL*, p. 209)
22 Kryten's big toe (*Infinity*, p. 194)
23 'A' Deck ('Camille')
24 Lister's books (*Infinity*, p. 171)
25 Rimmer's locker ('Balance of Power')
26 He took out a Brush-O-Matic and started 'doing' Lister's lapels ('Kryten')
27 She had been a Flight Engineer, Second Class, and was now aboard the *Nova 5*, a hologram (*Infinity*, p. 201)
28 Six weeks ('The Last Day' or *Infinity*, p. 32)
29 A thermos of nitro-glycerine ('Psirens')
30 A twenty-eighth-century derelict ('Out of Time')
31 Lister's piano in Better Than Life (*Infinity*, p. 267)
32 The guard Rimmer was manacled to when he was going to have his essence imprisoned (*BTL*, p. 51)
33 It rained herrings ('Confidence and Paranoia')
34 Treasurer ('Dimension Jump')
35 The twenty-fifth ('Rimmerworld')
36 When he was drunk before going into Better Than Life (*Infinity*, p. 294)
37 Seven hundred and ninety-three million (*Infinity*, p. 13)
38 The Io Amateur War Gamers and the Recreators of the Battle of Neasden Society ('Meltdown')
39 To the cinema ('Balance of Power')
40 Zero ('The End' or *Infinity*, p. 90)
41 In seventy-three hours and fourteen minutes (*Infinity*, p. 139)

The Answers

42 His armchair (*BTL*, p. 173)

43 Thirteen ('Justice')

44 Japanese, Mandarin and Satsuma ('Holoship')

45 Being hit ('Legion')

46 A sentence about a fearful, very bad estate agent going into a noxious toilet (*Infinity*, p. 145)

47 On top of a narrow metal locker in Corridor Omega 577 (*Infinity*, p. 216)

48 The side with the shortest haircuts ('Emohawk – Polymorph II')

49 Rimmer ('Quarantine')

50 'Goalpost head' (Rimmer) ('The Last Day')

51 Captain Yvette Richards (*Infinity*, p. 161)

52 When Dangerous Dan McGrew lost his skill ('Gunmen of the Apocalypse')

53 Seven (*BTL*, p. 15)

54 The two halves of the *Nova 5* (*Infinity*, p. 195)

55 Petersen ('The End')

56 4.30 a.m. ('Me²')

57 On its maiden voyage, on an excursion to the twentieth century ('Out of Time')

58 Hologramatic exercises for the dead ('Confidence and Paranoia')

59 242 (*Infinity*, p. 240)

60 Winnie-the-Pooh ('Meltdown')

61 Nirvanah Crane ('Holoship')

62 Death ('Emohawk – Polymorph II')

63 The *Nova 5*'s (*Infinity*, p. 163)

64 Made love to a woman ('Psirens')

65 Five ('Rimmerworld')

66 Seventeen ('Gunmen of the Apocalypse')

67 1 Corinthians 13 ('The Last Day')
68 Six (*Infinity*, p. 163)
69 17 July ('Me²')
70 4.30 a.m. (*Infinity*, p. 248)
71 The speed of reality ('Dimension Jump')
72 Gandalf the Master Wizard ('Terrorform')
73 Because he usually waited for the film to come out (*Infinity*, p. 149)
74 Thirty feet (*Infinity* p. 165)
75 On Lister's bedside cabinet when he was in hospital on the Backwards Planet (*BTL*, p. 220)
76 He copied the eye charts on to his shoes ('Rimmerworld')
77 Because his safety harness snapped and he fell into the cargo bay ('Balance of Power')
78 Kirsty Fantozi (*Infinity*, p. 175)
79 His right one ('The Inquisitor')
80 Twelve (*Infinity*, p. 217)
81 Country and Western ('Emohawk – Polymorph II')
82 To 16 August 1421 ('Out of Time')
83 From a *Red Dwarf* yearbook (*BTL*, p. 166)
84 $14.25 (*Infinity*, p. 259)
85 Rimmer's Hard Light Drive ('Legion')
86 The Cat's father ('Waiting for God')
87 3.37 a.m. (*Infinity*, p. 221)
88 The bank manager in Bedford Falls (*Infinity*, p. 260)
89 The cricket score ('The Last Day')
90 Sleeping (*BTL*, p. 119)
91 000169 ('The Inquisitor') or RD521169 ('Future Echoes')
92 In Lister's hankie ('Quarantine')

93 To stay in a nipple-covering position (*Infinity*, p. 274)
94 'Thou shalt not have more than ten suits' (*Infinity*, p. 128)
95 The Psirens' attempt to lure Lister ('Psirens')
96 'A grass skirt on a fat Hawaiian Hula-hoop champion' ('Emohawk – Polymorph II')
97 Sixty-seven minutes ('Terrorform')
98 Eight feet (*Infinity*, p. 262)
99 Floor 6120 ('Holoship')
100 Three (*BTL*, p. 187)
101 When he has to deprive an onion of its skin ('Out of Time')
102 Triton's (*Infinity*, p. 40)
103 An American game-show host ('Confidence and Paranoia')
104 Three hours (*BTL*, p. 203)
105 The Male Simulant ('Gunmen of the Apocalypse')
106 Rimmer and George S. Patton ('Legion')
107 A girl called Sandra (*Infinity*, p. 15)
108 Four zillion (*Infinity*, p. 131)

STAIRCASE 7

B	E	X	L	E	Y
S	A	T	U	R	N
M	O	N	K	E	Y
D	O	N	A	L	D
A	L	I	E	N	S
A	W	O	O	G	A

WORD SEARCH 7
Duane Dibbley

```
P O L Y M O R P H O Y A S T B A
D L N D S A D O A P S D O F O N
A K A E C L R A L I M A N F S I
S M G S P O T T L E U P J U B M
B A I P T A C D U D L I Q R I A
R S D A T I T E C D C A U D U L
I A R I D P C U I K O S N S E F
N I A R T S U S N T H N R A E O
Y K C Q P O O Q A S H T E D E O
L O H A I R C U T N B O T A M T
O A T F U N T I I O D M S O S P
N Q U I S D F D O A B A A L T R
J G E E K Y E E N U P T L A O I
O A D Y T P Q X I O P A P S V N
K C D U O I O U Q P T E N O I T
A T O O T H B R U S H S R E N C
R E R K C A P R O T A N O N U H
O A K D S I O R E R E C C O B A
N R O I V O N E I V Q R O S T R
A N N A A O T E P S O M R E H T
```

INSET

1 The Cat – the Riviera Kid (ace gunslinger); Lister – Brett Riverboat (knife thrower); Rimmer – Dangerous Dan McGrew (barefist fighting) ('Gunmen of the Apocalypse')
2 Duane Dibbley ('Emohawk – Polymorph II')
3 Lister ('Gunmen of the Apocalypse')
4 Kryten ('The Inquisitor')
5 Ninety-six per cent ('Holoship')
6 Cybernautics, Traffic Control ('Back to Reality')
7 Bear Strangler McGee's ('Gunmen of the Apocalypse')
8 'A rambling holiday through the diesel decks' ('Justice')
9 A fourteen-pound lump hammer ('White Hole')
10 *Big Boys in Boots*, July issue ('Dimension Jump')
11 He has a 'beautiful ass' ('The Inquisitor')
12 Seventeen hours ('Parallel Universe')
13 Sagittarius ('Parallel Universe')
14 Never ('The End'), three weeks ('Psirens') or just over a month (*Infinity*, p. 71)
15 Holly before going computer senile (*BTL*, p. 34)
16 The time-dilation formulae (*Infinity*, p. 85)

For information regarding BETTER THAN LIFE – the official UK RED DWARF Fan Club – readers should send an SAE to:

BETTER THAN LIFE,
40 Pitford Road,
Woodley,
Reading
Berks
RG5 4QF

READ MORE IN PENGUIN

The Making of Red Dwarf   Joe Nazzaro

Behind the scenes in deep space Shepperton, American journalist Joe Nazzaro spent three months with the *Red Dwarf* cast and crew during the shooting of Series VI.

This a fascinating account of how an ambitious and technically complex TV show is translated from script to screen, together with interviews and observations from the stars, writers, producers and production team.

How close are the stars to their real characters?

Where do the ideas for the series come from?

Are the multi-award-winning model sequences really shot in outer space?

Packed with stunning behind-the-scenes photographs, with an introduction by the series' creators Rob Grant and Doug Naylor, this book is not only an unmissable treat for *Red Dwarf* fans, but a valuable reference work on how a television series is made.

The Man in the Rubber Mask   Robert Llewellyn

Following smash-hit (well, pretty successful) appearances in the West End and at the Edinburgh Festival, Robert Llewellyn – actor, writer, alternative comedian and sometimes nude model – was plucked from the heights of fame by the unstoppable forces of Grant Naylor. His punishment: to spend the rest of his days encased in a latex rubber mask in the BBC special effects department in darkest Acton, cast as the robot Kryten in *Red Dwarf*.

The Man in the Rubber Mask is nothing less than a devastating account of the terrors, trials and tribulations of the making of *Red Dwarf*! Nothing less than a guidebook to the biggest cult series in the Universe!

READ MORE IN PENGUIN

Red Dwarf   Grant Naylor

When Lister got drunk, he got really drunk.

After celebrating his birthday with a Monopoly-board pub crawl around London, he came to in a burger bar on one of Saturn's moons, wearing a lady's pink crimplene hat and a pair of yellow fishing waders, with no money and a passport in the name of 'Emily Berkenstein'.

Joining the Space Corps seemed a good idea. *Red Dwarf*, a clapped-out spaceship, was bound for Earth. It never made it, leaving Lister as the last remaining member of the human race, three million years from Earth, with only a dead man, a senile computer and highly evolved cat for company.

They begin their journey home. On the way they'll break the Light Barrier. They'll meet Einstein, Archimedes, God and Norman Wisdom . . . and discover an alternative plane of Reality.

Primordial Soup   Grant Naylor

Before recorded Time, there existed a substance known as Primordial Soup. From this disgustingly unpromising, gunky substance, all life began. Likewise, from the disgustingly unpromising, gunky scripts, sprang the disgusting, gunky comedy series, *Red Dwarf*.

Primordial Soup is a selection of the least worst scripts from the first five years of *Red Dwarf*, tracing the series from its humble beginnings to its humble present.

Each of the scripts has been personally chosen by the author from his rubber-sheeted bed in the Norfolk Nursing Home of the Intellectually Challenged.

READ MORE IN PENGUIN

Better Than Life   Grant Naylor

Lister is lost. Three million years from Earth he's marooned in a world created by his own psyche. For Lister it's the most dangerous place he could possibly be because he's completely happy.

Rimmer has a problem too. He's dead. But that's not the problem. Rimmer's problem is that he's trapped in a landscape controlled by his own subconscious. And Rimmer's subconscious doesn't like him one little bit.

Together with Cat, the best-dressed entity in all six known universes, and Kryten, a sanitation Mechanoid with a missing sanity chip, they are trapped in the ultimate computer game: Better Than Life. The zenith of computer-game technology, BTL transports you directly to a perfect world of your imagination, a world where you can enjoy fabulous wealth and unmitigated success.

It's the ideal game with only one drawback – it's so good, it will kill you.

and

The Red Dwarf Omnibus